THE MAGIC OF
HEBREW
CHANT
COMPANION

The Big Book of Musical Notations and Incantations

The musical notations companion to *The Magic of Hebrew Chant: Healing the Spirit, Transforming the Mind, Deepening Love* by Rabbi Shefa Gold.

RABBI SHEFA GOLD

Transcribed by Cantor Audrey Abrams with James Cooper

Other Spiritual Practice Resources
Available from Jewish Lights

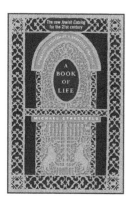  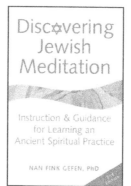  

THE MAGIC OF
HEBREW
CHANT
COMPANION

The Big Book of Musical Notations and Incantations

RABBI SHEFA GOLD

Transcribed by Cantor Audrey Abrams with James Cooper

For People of All Faiths, All Backgrounds
JEWISH LIGHTS Publishing
Nashville, Tennessee
www.jewishlights.com

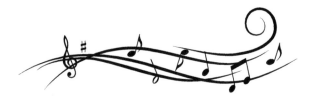

The Magic of Hebrew Chant Companion:
The Big Book of Musical Notations and Incantations

ISBN: 978-1-58023-722-2 Spiralbound
ISBN: 978-1-68336-651-5 Paperback

Manufactured in the United States of America

For People of All Faiths, All Backgrounds
Jewish Lights Publishing
An imprint of Turner Publishing Company
4507 Charlotte Avenue, Suite 100
Nashville, TN 37209
Tel: (615) 255-2665
www.jewishlights.com

Contents

SCRIPTURE

𝒫SALMS

THE DAILY PSALMS

ISAIAH

Introduction

I have been blessed to be the channel for an abundant flow of melodies, which have found their way across the world. Sometimes I get letters from travelers who write and say, "Shefa, I heard your song being sung in Moscow! In Havana! In Uruguay!" Or I travel somewhere and hear a chant I composed twenty years ago and the community is sure that it is "*miSinai*" (brought down from Mount Sinai with the Torah) ... and they'll even tell me I'm singing it wrong! Or sitting in a pew at B'nai Jeshurun in New York City, I join over one thousand worshipers in singing my chant *Mah Gadlu*.

I love it ... and yet, there is a deep yearning in me to dedicate the power of these melodies as spiritual practices that can evolve over a lifetime and keep taking us deeper and deeper. The words and melody are powerful by themselves, but they are just the surface.

In *The Magic of Hebrew Chant: Healing the Spirit, Transforming the Mind, Deepening Love* I explore the theory about what chanting is and how to use chant for healing, inquiry, and connection with the deepest mysteries. I present over one hundred spiritual practices and the specific intentions for each of them. This musical companion presents those spiritual practices in a larger format, perfect for the individual musician and group use. I am so grateful to be able to present these melodies to you. I hope that you will use them as incantations or as vehicles for transport as you explore the far reaches of consciousness and the depths of the heart.

You can think of each of these melodies as a *Mishkan*, a place where the Divine Presence can be invited to enter. In building the *Mishkan*, we must gather up all of our talent, power, intuition, skills, vision, imagination, and musicality and dedicate all of the beauty and force of the chant to the possibility of creating a home for *Shechinah*.

The *Mishkan* is portable; we carry it with us through the wilderness of our lives so that we will always have access to the inner mysteries.

God says, "*V'asu li mikdash v'shachanti b'tocham*. Make for me a holy place so that I can dwell among, between, and within you" (Exodus 25:8). In the book of Exodus, we find detailed instruction for the building of the *Mishkan*. Only those with willing, generous hearts are allowed to contribute to this endeavor. We bring the most exquisite colors, jewels, fragrance ... all of our finest artistry to this project, and then all of this beauty is dedicated as a nexus between human and Divine, between heaven and earth. In the end, the important part is not the outer form, but what is inside, for that is where God speaks to us. The farther within you get, the more holy is the space.

As you learn these melodies, you can use their outer forms to send you to that holy innerness.

These exquisitely detailed *Mishkan* texts of Exodus are interrupted by a story that is meant as a warning for our ancestors and for us. The people get nervous when Moses is up on the mountain for such a long time, and they ask Aaron to make them a Golden Calf, so they can worship. This turns out to be a big mistake with dire consequences.

The Golden Calf became synonymous with idolatry. And idolatry is understood by our tradition as the root of all our mistakes.

Well, when you think about it, what is the difference between a *Mishkan* and a Golden Calf? While the *Mishkan* is meant to send us to the beyond that is within, the Golden Calf is solid, existing of and for itself. We supply the gold, but then the Calf seems to take on a life of its own. Aaron describes the process, saying, "I cast the gold into the fire and out came this calf!" (Exodus 32:24). The Calf has no interior space. It glorifies itself. It is "full of itself." It represents the most dangerous hindrance in the life of spiritual practice: that of worshiping and staying attached to the forms, rather than allowing those forms to send us inward to the essence, as is their purpose.

The difference between building a *Mishkan* and building a Golden Calf is sometimes very subtle. Sometimes I really think I'm building a *Mishkan*, but then my habitual egoic manipulations ... my ambitions, attachments, pride, vanity, or arrogance seep in. Quite suddenly I find myself in the presence of a very beautiful and seductive Golden Calf. When I realize this, I can usually find my way back to *Mishkan* and again be sent to the infinite mystery within.

As you learn these chants, or create your own, just remember to keep asking, "Am I building a *Mishkan* or a Golden Calf?"

In composing a chant, I don't take a text and put it to music. I become intimate with a text, and the music is born out of this intimacy. I hope that when you chant these sacred words, these simple melodies, you too will be drawn into an intimate relationship with the text, with the ancestors who left these words for us as gifts to unwrap, with your own deepest desires, and with God, the Great Mystery, who is waiting for us with open arms.

As you learn these melodies, let them live inside you. The notes are just the bare bones. It's up to you to give them flesh and blood and spirit, so feel free to interpret them as you wish. (If you'd like to hear my interpretation, you can find most of these on my website: www.RabbiShefaGold.com). It will be your responsibility to learn the notes carefully before you decide to improvise. What is sometimes called "folk process" is often just carelessness.

Once someone asked Reb Shlomo Carlebach if it was OK to change a melody he had composed. After all, what did it matter? Reb Shlomo answered with a story:

> A young man went to a party and met the most beautiful woman he had ever encountered. She was perfect—sweet and smart, sexy and loving. She gave him her telephone number. When the young man got home he looked at the number and said, "Hmmm, I don't like this number so much ... I think I'll change this '3' to a '4.' I think this number is better."

May these melodies connect you to the Beloved. May they become the vehicles for the best in you to be carried into the world.

LITURGY

AWAKENING

מוֹדֶה אֲנִי לְפָנֶיךָ

Modeh ani l'fanecha.
I gratefully acknowledge Your face.
(from the morning liturgy)

Shefa Gold

Mo-deh a-ni l'-fa-ne-cha.   Mo-deh a-ni l'-fa-ne - cha.   Mo-deh a-ni l'-fa ne - cha.

CLEARING THE WAY

אָנָּא, בְּכֹחַ גְּדֻלַּת יְמִינְךָ, תַּתִּיר צְרוּרָה

Ana b'choach g'dulat y'min'cha tatir tz'rurah.
Please, with the strength of your right hand, untie our tangles.

Shefa Gold

A - na b'-cho - ach g' - du - lat y' - min' - cha   ta - tir   tz' - ru - rah

ta - tir   tz' - ru - rah.   A - na b'-cho - ach g' - du - lat y' - min' - cha

ta - tir   tz' - ru - rah   ta - tir   tz' - ru - rah.

3

BETROTHAL:
THE SEVEN CHANNELS OF COMMITMENT

וְאֵרַשְׂתִּיךְ לִי לְעוֹלָם

וְאֵרַשְׂתִּיךְ לִי בְּצֶדֶק

וּבְמִשְׁפָּט

וּבְחֶסֶד

וּבְרַחֲמִים

וְאֵרַשְׂתִּיךְ לִי בֶּאֱמוּנָה

וְיָדַעַתְּ אֶת־יהוה

V'eirastich li l'olam, v'eirastich li b'tzedek, uv'mishpat, uv'chesed, uv'rachamim.
V'eirastich li be'emunah, v'yada'at et Yah.
I will betroth you to Me forever, I will betroth you to Me with justice,
and with impeccability, and with love, and with compassion.
I will betroth you to Me in faith. And then you will know [be intimate with] God.
(Hosea 2:21–22)

Shefa Gold

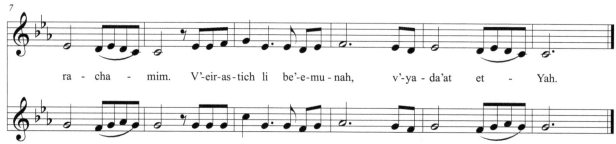

GRATEFULNESS

אוֹדְךָ בְּעוֹד תִּהְיֶה נִשְׁמַת אֱלוֹהַ בִּי

Odach b'od t'h'yeh nishmat Eloha bi.
I will thank You as long as the divine breath is in me.
(Solomon ibn Gabirol, eleventh-century Spanish poet and philosopher)

Shefa Gold

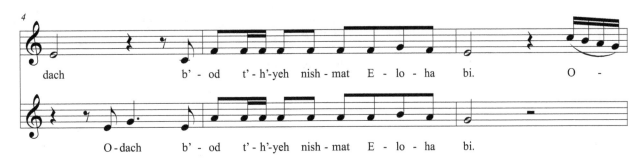

O WONDROUS HEALER

רוֹפֵא כָל בָּשָׂר וּמַפְלִיא לַעֲשׂוֹת

Rofei chol basar umafli la'asot!

O wondrous Healer of all flesh!

(from the morning liturgy)

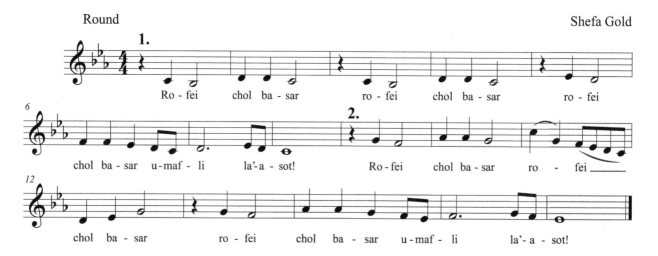

GATHERING IN

וַהֲבִיאֵנוּ לְשָׁלוֹם מֵאַרְבַּע כַּנְפוֹת הָאָרֶץ

V'havi'einu l'shalom mei'arba kanfot ha'aretz.

(Bring us in peace from the four corners of the earth.)

Uriel! Micha'el! Rafa'el! Gavri'el!

Shefa Gold

O PURE SOUL

אֱלֹהַי, נְשָׁמָה שֶׁנָּתַתָּ בִּי טְהוֹרָה הִיא

Elohai n'shamah shenatata bi t'horah hi.
O pure soul, in you I see endless possibility!
(liturgy)

Shefa Gold

MORNING BLESSINGS

O God, who sets the captive free, who opens the eyes of the blind to see,
who heals the lame and loves the just. I will praise Yah with my life!
(Psalm 146:7–8, 146:2)

אֲהַלְלָה יהוה בְּחַיָּי

Ahal'lah Yah b'chayai!
I will praise Yah with my life!
(Psalm 146:2)

יהוה מַתִּיר אֲסוּרִים
יהוה פֹּקֵחַ עִוְרִים
יהוה זֹקֵף כְּפוּפִים
יהוה אֹהֵב צַדִּיקִים

Adonai matir asurim, Adonai pokei'ach ivrim,
Adonai zokeif k'fufim, Adonai oheiv tzadikim.

HOLY SPEECH

בָּרוּךְ שֶׁאָמַר וְהָיָה הָעוֹלָם

Baruch she'amar v'hayah ha'olam.

Blessed is the One who speaks the world into being.

Shefa Gold

ASHREI

אַשְׁרֵי יוֹשְׁבֵי בֵיתֶךָ עוֹד יְהַלְלוּךָ

Ashrei yosh'vei veitecha od y'hal'lucha.
Happy are those who dwell in Your house; they keep on praising.
(Psalm 84:5)

Shefa Gold

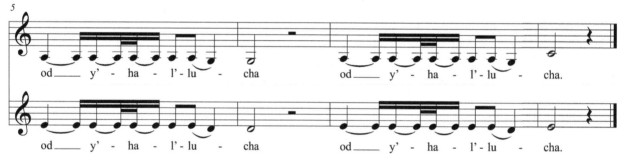

MANIFESTING TORAH

לִלְמֹד וּלְלַמֵּד, לִשְׁמֹר וְלַעֲשׂוֹת וּלְקַיֵּם

Lilmod ul'lameid lishmor v'la'asot ul'kayeim.

To learn and to teach, to uphold and to practice and to manifest.

Shefa Gold

GOODNESS

הוֹדוּ לַיהוה כִּי־טוֹב כִּי לְעוֹלָם חַסְדּוֹ

Hodu ladonai ki tov, ki l'olam chasdo.

Give thanks to God for essential goodness; His kindness endures forever.

(Psalm 136:1)

Shefa Gold

EYES, HEARTS, AND HANDS

וְהָאֵר עֵינֵינוּ בְּתוֹרָתֶךָ, וְדַבֵּק לִבֵּנוּ בְּמִצְוֹתֶיךָ

V'ha'eir eineinu b'Toratecha, v'dabeik libeinu b'mitzvotecha.

Enlighten our eyes with Your Torah, and connect our hearts to Your *mitzvot*.

Shefa Gold

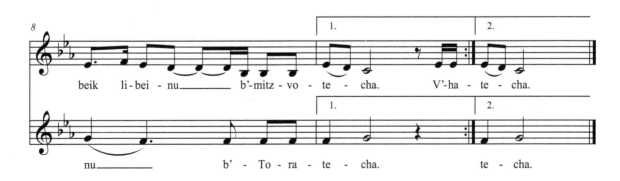

SHEHECHEYANU:
A MEDITATION ON THIS MOMENT

שֶׁהֶחֱיָנוּ וְקִיְּמָנוּ וְהִגִּיעָנוּ לַזְּמַן הַזֶּה

Shehecheyanu, v'kiy'manu, v'higianu laz'man hazeh.
O Mystery, Grace unfolding, O Miracle, it's You alone,
O Mystery, Grace unfolding, O Miracle, who brings us Home.

UNIFYING THE HEART

וְיַחֵד לְבָבֵנוּ לְאַהֲבָה וּלְיִרְאָה אֶת שְׁמֶךָ

V'yacheid l'vaveinu l'ahavah ul'yirah et sh'mecha.

Unify our hearts to love and to be in awe of Your name/essence.

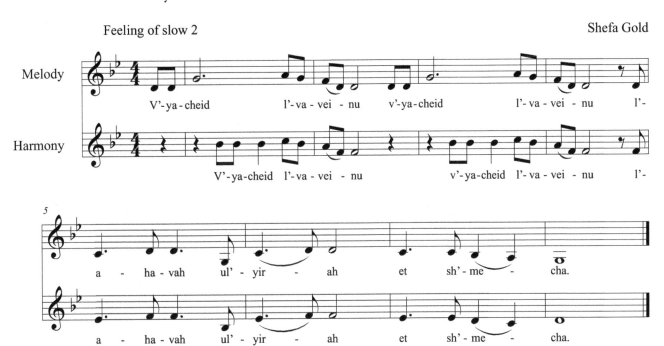

INCANTATION FOR HOPEFULNESS

לִישׁוּעָתְךָ קִוִּיתִי יְהוֹה; קִוִּיתִי יְהוֹה לִישׁוּעָתְךָ;
יְהוֹה לִישׁוּעָתְךָ קִוִּיתִי

Lishuatcha kiviti Yah; kiviti Yah lishuatcha; Yah lishuatcha kiviti.
I wait/hope for Your salvation.
(Genesis 49:18; bedtime liturgy)

Shefa Gold

UNDER THE WINGS

וַאֲנִי מָצָאתִי מְנוּחָה מִתַּחַת כַּנְפֵי הַשְּׁכִינָה

Va'ani matzati m'nuchah mitachat kanfei HaShechinah.
Under the wings of *Shechinah* I have found my rest.

Shefa Gold

FREEDOM AND HOMECOMING:
A CHANT FOR ROSH HASHANAH

תְּקַע בְּשׁוֹפָר גָּדוֹל לְחֵרוּתֵנוּ, וְשָׂא נֵס לְקַבֵּץ גָּלֻיוֹתֵינוּ

T'ka b'shofar gadol l'cheiruteinu, v'sa neis l'kabeitz galuyoteinu.
Sound the great shofar for our freedom,
and raise the banner as we all come home.

Shefa Gold

CHANUKAH CHANT

Let the flame be kindled within me, let Your love burn bright,
I hunger for Your light, I hunger for Your light.

Shefa Gold

PILGRIMAGE

לִירוּשָׁלַיִם עִירְךָ בְּרַחֲמִים תָּשׁוּב

Li'Y'rushalayim ircha, b'rachamim tashuv.

To Jerusalem Your city, with compassion you will return.

(from the daily *Amidah*)

Shefa Gold

USHPIZIN

תִּיבוּ תִּיבוּ אוּשְׁפִּיזִין עִלָּאִין,

תִּיבוּ תִּיבוּ אוּשְׁפִּיזִין קַדִּישִׁין

Tivu tivu ushpizin ila'in, tivu tivu ushpizin kadishin.

Sit down, sit down, exalted guests; sit down, sit down, holy guests!

Shefa Gold

ALL IS ONE

אַתָּה אֶחָד וְשִׁמְךָ אֶחָד

Atah Echad v'shimcha Echad.
You are One and Your name/essence is One.

מְנוּחַת אַהֲבָה וּנְדָבָה

M'nuchat ahavah un'davah.
Rest of love and generosity.

מְנוּחַת אֱמֶת וֶאֱמוּנָה

M'nuchat emet ve'emunah.
Rest of truth and faith.

מְנוּחַת שָׁלוֹם וְשַׁלְוָה

M'nuchat shalom v'shalvah.
Rest of peace and serenity.

מְנוּחָה שְׁלֵמָה שֶׁאַתָּה רוֹצֶה בָּהּ

M'nuchat sh'leimah she'atah rotzeh bah.
A perfect rest in which You find favor.

Shefa Gold

Verse 3: *M'nuchat emet ve'emunah.* All is One.
Verse 4: *M'nuchat shalom v'shalvah.* All is One.
Verse 5: *M'nuchat sh'leimah she'atah rotzeh bah.* All is One.
Verse 6: *Atah Echad v'shimcha Echad.* All is One.

ROLLING

גּוֹלֵל אוֹר מִפְּנֵי חֹשֶׁךְ, וְחֹשֶׁךְ מִפְּנֵי אוֹר

Goleil or mipnei choshech, v'choshech mipnei or.
Rolling away light before darkness, darkness before light.
(from the evening liturgy)

Shefa Gold

LIFE AND DEATH

כִּי אַתָּה מְחַיֶּה הַמֵּתִים וּמֵמִית חַיִּים

Ki atah m'chayeih hameitim, umeimit chayim.
For You revive the dead and bring death to the living.
(from the *Taharah* liturgy)

Shefa Gold

SIM SHALOM

שִׂים שָׁלוֹם טוֹבָה וּבְרָכָה, חֵן וָחֶסֶד וְרַחֲמִים

Sim shalom tovah uv'rachah chein vachesed v'rachamim!
Grant us peace, goodness, grace, love, and compassion!

Round

Shefa Gold

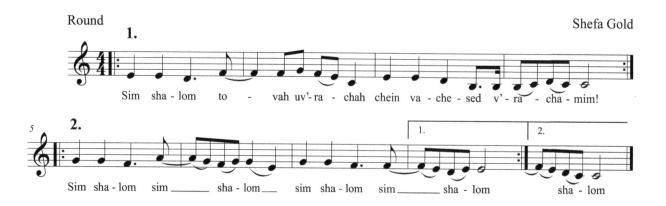

THE SAVING POWER OF GOD-CONSCIOUSNESS

שִׁירוּ לַיהוה כָּל־הָאָרֶץ

בַּשְּׂרוּ מִיּוֹם־אֶל־יוֹם יְשׁוּעָתוֹ

Shiru l'Adonai kol ha'aretz, bas'ru miyom el yom y'shuato!

Shiru la'Shechinah kol ha'aretz, bas'ru miyom el yom y'shuata!

Hallelu, Hallelu, Hallelu, Hallelu, Hallelu, HalleluYah!

Sing to the Lord, everyone on earth, announce His salvation daily!

Sing to the indwelling Divine Presence, announce Her salvation daily!

Praise Yah!

(1 Chronicles 16:23; Psalm 96:2)

Shefa Gold

THE MEDICINE FOR OVERWHELM: TACHANUN

וְהוּא רַחוּם

V'hu rachum.

It is compassionate.

נִבְהֲלָה נַפְשֵׁנוּ מֵרֹב עִצְּבוֹנֵנוּ,

Nivhalah nafsheinu meirov itzvoneinu. (2x)

אַל תִּשְׁכָּחֵנוּ נֶצַח

Al tishkacheinu netzach. (2x)

קוּמָה וְהוֹשִׁיעֵנוּ, כִּי חָסִינוּ בָךְ

Kumah v'hoshi'einu ki chasinu vach! (2x)

Our soul trembles, overwhelmed by sadness,

do not forget us, arise and save us, for we take shelter in You!

Shefa Gold

do not for - get us,____ arise ____ and save us,____ for we take

shel - ter in You! We take shel - ter in You! Arise

____ and save us,____ for we take shel - ter in You! We take shel - ter in You!

D.C. al Fine

BALANCING WILL AND SURRENDER

עָזִּי וְזִמְרָת יָהּ וַיְהִי־לִי לִישׁוּעָה

Ozi v'zimrat Yah vay'hi li lishuah.

My strength (balanced) with the song of God will be my salvation.

(Psalm 118:14; Exodus 15:2)

Round

Shefa Gold

O - zi____ v'-zim - rat Yah____ va-y'-hi li____ li-shu - ah. O -

zi____ v'-zim - rat Yah____ va-y'hi li____ li-shu - ah. O -

zi____ v'-zim-rat Yah____ va-y'-hi li____ li-shu - ah. O - zi____ v'-zim-rat

Yah____ va-y'-hi li_____ li-shu - ah. O -

THE MAJESTY OF NURTURE

לְתַקֵּן עוֹלָם בְּמַלְכוּת שַׁדַּי

L'takein olam b'malchut Shaddai.
Healing the world through the Majesty of Nurture.
(liturgy)

Shefa Gold

BLESSING OF MY SOUL

בָּרְכִי נַפְשִׁי אֶת יהוה, הַלְלוּיָהּ

Bar'chi nafshi et Adonai, halleluyah!
Bless the place of Sovereignty, O my soul!

Round

Shefa Gold

Bar'-chi naf-shi et A-do-nai,_____ Bar'-chi naf-shi et A-do-nai,_____

et A-do-nai,_____ ha-le-lu ha-le-lu ha-le-lu ha-le-lu ha-le-lu-u-u Yah!____ Ha-le-

lu ha-le-lu ha-le-lu ha-le-lu ha-le-lu-u-u Yah.____ Ha-le-lu-u-u Yah!____

STANDING BEFORE THE MYSTERY

דַּע לִפְנֵי מִי אַתָּה עוֹמֵד

Da lifnei mi atah omeid!
Know before whom you stand!
(adapted from Talmud, *B'rachot 28b*)

Round

Shefa Gold

Da lif-nei mi a-tah o-meid!____ Da lif-nei mi a-

tah____ o-meid! Da lif-nei mi a-tah o-meid!____

Da lif-nei mi a-tah o-meid! tah____ o-meid!

BEINI UVEIN

בֵּינִי וּבֵין בְּנֵי יִשְׂרָאֵל אוֹת הִוא לְעֹלָם
כִּי־שֵׁשֶׁת יָמִים עָשָׂה יהוה אֶת־הַשָּׁמַיִם
וְאֶת־הָאָרֶץ וּבַיּוֹם הַשְּׁבִיעִי שָׁבַת וַיִּנָּפַשׁ

Beini uvein b'nei Yisrael ot hi l'olam ki sheishet yamim asah Adonai et hashamayim v'et ha'aretz
uvayom hash'vi'i shavat vayinafash!
Let it be a sign between us forever, for in six days I made everything
and on the seventh day I made Shabbat, I made Shabbat for my Soul!
(Exodus 31:17)

Shefa Gold

Soul! Hai dai lai lai lai dai hai dia lai lai lai dai hai dai lai lai lai

dai hai dai lai lai lai dai_____ Soul! I made Shab-bat for my Soul!

SUKKAT SHALOM

הַשְׁכִּיבֵנוּ יהוה אֱלֹהֵינוּ לְשָׁלוֹם,

וְהַעֲמִידֵנוּ מַלְכֵּנוּ לְחַיִּים טוֹבִים וּלְשָׁלוֹם,

וּפְרוֹשׂ עָלֵינוּ סֻכַּת שְׁלוֹמֶךָ

Hashkiveinu Adonai Eloheinu l'shalom.

V'ha'amideinu Malkeinu, l'chayim tovim ul'shalom.

Uf'ros Aleinu sukkat sh'lomecha.

O Lord, our God, let us lie down in peace.

Our Sovereign, raise us up again to good life and peace.

Spread over us a shelter of peace.

(liturgy)

Shefa Gold

Hash - ki-vei - nu A - do - nai E - lo - hei - nu
V'ha' - ami-dei - nu Mal - kei - nu l'cha - yim___ to - vim

1. l' - sha - lom. 2. u - l' sha - lom. U -

f'ros A - lei - nu suk - kat sh'lo - me - cha. 1. U - 2. me - cha.

SURRENDER

בְּיָדְךָ אַפְקִיד רוּחִי, בְּעֵת אִישָׁן וְאָעִירָה
וְעִם רוּחִי גְּוִיָּתִי, יהוה לִי וְלֹא אִירָא

B'yad'cha af'kid ruchi, b'ayt ishan v'a-ira,
v'im ruchi g'vi-ati, Adonai li v'lo ira.
Into Your hand I entrust my spirit, when I sleep and when I awaken,
when spirit is with my body, God is with me; I will not fear.
(the last lines of *Adon Olam*, attributed to Solomon ibn Gavirol)

call and response

Shefa Gold

do - nai li - - - - - v' - lo i - ra   b' -

do - nai li - - - - - v' - lo i - ra   b' -

GOING UP WITH JOY
וְשָׁם נָשִׁיר שִׁיר חָדָשׁ וּבִרְנָנָה נַעֲלֶה

V'sham nashir shir chadash uvir'nanah na'aleh.
And there we will sing a new song; with joy we will go up.
(from *Tzur Mishelo*)

Shefa Gold

Melody

V' - sham na - shir   shir   cha - dash   u - vir' - na - nah____ na' - a -

Harmony

leh.   V' - vir' - na - nah____ na' - a - leh.

SCRIPTURE

KNOWING BEAUTY AND
FINDING THE UNIVERSE
אֶת־הַכֹּל עָשָׂה יָפֶה בְעִתּוֹ גַּם אֶת־הָעֹלָם נָתַן בְּלִבָּם

Et hakol asah yafeh v'ito, gam et ha'olam natan b'libam.
[God] makes everything beautiful in its time,
and also hides the universe in their hearts.
(Ecclesiastes 3:11)

Round

Shefa Gold

Et ha - kol a - sah_____ ya - feh v'-i-to,_____ gam et ha-o-lam___ na-

tan b'-li - bam,___ gam et ha'-o - lam___ na - tan b'-li - bam.

AN OATH OF FRIENDSHIP
הִנֵּה יהוה בֵּינִי וּבֵינְךָ עַד־עוֹלָם

Hineih Yah beini uveincha, ad olam!
Here is God between me and you forever!
(1 Samuel 20:23)

Round

Shefa Gold

Hi - neih___ Yah___ bei - ni u - vein -cha, hi - neih___ Yah___ bei - ni u - vein -cha,

ad _____ o - lam _____ ad _____ o - lam!

HOLY GROUND

אַדְמַת־קֹדֶשׁ הוּא

Admat kodesh hu!
It is holy ground!
(Exodus 3:5)

Round   Shefa Gold

GO WITHIN US

יֵלֶךְ־נָא אֲדֹנָי בְּקִרְבֵּנוּ

Yeilech na Adonai b'kirbeinu.
Please, God, go within us.
(Exodus 34:9)

Round   Shefa Gold

ASCENDING
וְעַל בָּמוֹתַי יַדְרִכֵנִי

V'al bamotai yadricheini.
He prepares a path for me upon the high places.
(Habakkuk 3:19)

Shefa Gold

OPENING TO THE SOURCE OF FLOW
וְנָהָר יֹצֵא מֵעֵדֶן לְהַשְׁקוֹת אֶת־הַגָּן

V'nahar yotzei mei'Eden, l'hashkot et hagan.
A river comes forth from Eden to water the garden.
(Genesis 2:10)

Shefa Gold

BELOVED

אֲנִי לְדוֹדִי וְדוֹדִי לִי

Ani l'Dodi v'Dodi li.
I am my Beloved's and my Beloved is mine.
(Song of Songs 6:3)

Shefa Gold

HOW BEAUTIFUL!

הִנָּךְ יָפָה רַעְיָתִי הִנָּךְ יָפָה

Hinach yafah rayati, hinach yafah!
How beautiful You are, my Friend, how beautiful!
(Song of Songs 1:15)

Freely

Shefa Gold

Hi-nach ya - fah ra-ya-ti, hi - nach ya - fah! Hi-nach ya -

fah ra-ya-ti, hi - nach ya - fah! Hi-nach ya - fah ra-ya-ti,

hi - nach ya - fah! Hi-nach ya - fah ra-ya-ti, hi - nach ya - fah!

AN APPETITE FOR HOLINESS

וּבָא בְּכָל־אַוַּת נַפְשׁוֹ אֶל־הַמָּקוֹם

U-va-a-a b'chol avat nafsho el HaMakom.
And he [the Levite] shall come with all the desire of his soul to the Place.
(Deuteronomy 18:6)

Round

Shefa Gold

U - va - a - a b'chol a - vat naf - sho el Ha-Ma - kom. U-

va - a - a b'chol a - vat naf - sho el Ha-Ma - kom. U -

IN HIS SHADE

בְּצִלּוֹ חִמַּדְתִּי וְיָשַׁבְתִּי וּפִרְיוֹ מָתוֹק לְחִכִּי

B'tzilo chimadti v'yashavti, ufiryo matok l'chiki.
In His shade I delight to sit, tasting His sweet fruit.
(Song of Songs 2:3)

Shefa Gold

COME, MY BELOVED

לְכָה דוֹדִי נֵצֵא הַשָּׂדֶה

L'cha Dodi neitzeih hasadeh.

Come, my Beloved, let us go out to the field.

(Song of Songs 7:12)

Shefa Gold

LOVING "THIS"

זֶה דוֹדִי וְזֶה רֵעִי

Zeh Dodi v'zeh Rei'i.
This is my Beloved; this is my Friend.
(Song of Songs 5:16)

Shefa Gold

HOW AWESOME!

מַה־נּוֹרָא הַמָּקוֹם הַזֶּה

Mah nora HaMakom hazeh!

How awesome is this place!

(Genesis 28:17)

Shefa Gold

LISTENING TO THE VOICE OF WISDOM #1

הֲלֹא־חָכְמָה תִקְרָא וּתְבוּנָה תִּתֵּן קוֹלָהּ

Halo chochmah tikra, ut'vunah titein kolah!
Isn't it Wisdom calling and Understanding raising her voice!
(Proverbs 8:1)

Shefa Gold

Ha - lo choch - mah tik - ra,_____ u - t'- vu - nah ti -

tein ko - lah!_____ Ha- Ha - lo choch - mah tik - ra,_____

_____ u - t'-vu - nah ti - tein ko - lah!_____ Ha- tein ko - lah!_____

LISTENING TO THE VOICE OF WISDOM #2

אַשְׁרֵי אָדָם שֹׁמֵעַ לִי

Ashrei adam shomei'a li.
Happy is the one who listens to me.
(Proverbs 8:34)

Shefa Gold

Voice 1   Ash - rei a-dam sho -mei'-a li, sho - mei' - a li.

Voice 2   Ash - rei a-dam ash - rei a - dam_____ sho - mei' - a li._____

Voice 3   Ash - rei a-dam ash - rei a - dam_____ sho - mei' - a li.

SOUL LIGHT

נֵר יהוה נִשְׁמַת אָדָם חֹפֵשׂ כָּל חַדְרֵי בָטֶן

Neir Adonai nishmat adam chofeis kol chadrei vaten.
My soul is the flame of God that searches the inner chambers.
(Proverbs 20:27)

Round (up to 8 parts)

Shefa Gold

THE REWARDS OF OUR ATTENTION

נֹצֵר תְּאֵנָה יֹאכַל פִּרְיָהּ

Notzeir t'einah yochal piryah.
Those who guard the truth will be nourished by her fruit.
(Proverbs 27:18)

Shefa Gold

AWAKENING COMPASSION
מִי יָכִין לָעֹרֵב צֵידוֹ כִּי־יְלָדָו אֶל־אֵל יְשַׁוֵּעוּ

Mi yachin la'oreiv tzeido ki y'ladav el El y'shavei'u?
Who prepares nourishment for the raven
when its young ones call out to God?
(Job 38:41)

Shefa Gold

Mi ya-chin la'-o-reiv tzei-do___ ki y'-la-dav el El y'-sha-vei'-u?

dav el El y'-sha-vei'-u? Mi ya-chin la'-o-reiv tzei-do___ ki y'-la-dav el El y'-sha-vei'-

u? dav el El y'-sha-vei'-u?

PRAISE: THE FORCE OF HEALING AND SALVATION
רְפָאֵנִי יהוה וְאֵרָפֵא הוֹשִׁיעֵנִי וְאִוָּשֵׁעָה כִּי תְהִלָּתִי אָתָּה

R'fa'eini Yah v'eirafei; hoshi'eini v'ivashei'ah ki t'hilati atah.
Heal me, God, and I will be healed; save me and I will be saved ...
for my praise is You.
(Jeremiah 17:14)

Shefa Gold

R'fa-ei-ni Yah v'-ei-ra-fei; ho-shi'-ei-ni v'-i-va-shei'-ah

ki t'-hi-la-ti___ a-tah, ki t'-hi-la-ti___ a-tah.

PLANTING AND HARVEST

וְנָטְעוּ כְרָמִים וְשָׁתוּ אֶת־יֵינָם
וְעָשׂוּ גַנּוֹת וְאָכְלוּ אֶת־פְּרִיהֶם

V'nat'u ch'ramim v'shatu et yeinam,

v'asu ganot v'achlu et p'rihem.

And they will plant vineyards and drink the wine thereof,

And they shall make gardens and eat the fruit of them.

(Amos 9:14)

Round

Shefa Gold

V'-nat'-u ch'-ra-mim v'-sha-tu et yei-nam,

v'-a-su ga-not v'-ach-lu et p'ri-hem.

CRYING OUT TO GOD

אִם־כֵּן לָמָּה זֶּה אָנֹכִי

Im kein, lamah zeh anochi?

If this is the way it is, why am I?

(Genesis 25:22)

Shefa Gold

Im kein, la-mah zeh a-no-chi? Im kein, la-mah

zeh a-no-chi, la-mah zeh a-no-chi? Im kein, Im

6 part round - new part enter at each measure

A NEW COVENANT

נָתַתִּי אֶת־תּוֹרָתִי בְּקִרְבָּם וְעַל־לִבָּם אֶכְתָּבֶנָּה

Natati et Torati b'kirbam, v'al libam echtavenah.
I will put my Torah into their inmost being and
inscribe it upon their hearts.
(Jeremiah 31:33)

Shefa Gold

RUTH

עַמֵּךְ עַמִּי וֵאלֹהַיִךְ אֱלֹהָי

Ameich ami veilohayich Elohai.

Your people are my people, and your God is my God.

(Ruth 1:16)

Shefa Gold

FIRE ON THE ALTAR

אֵשׁ תָּמִיד תּוּקַד עַל־הַמִּזְבֵּחַ לֹא תִכְבֶּה

Aish tamid tukad al hamizbayach; lo tichbeh.
Fire always shall be kept burning on the altar; it shall not go out.
(Leviticus 6:6)

Shefa Gold

PSALMS

INVITING OUR FUTURE SELVES

הוֹדִיעֵנִי יהוה   קִצִּי וּמִדַּת יָמַי מַה־הִיא

Hodi'eiani Yah kitzi, umidat yamai mah hi?
O God, show me my end, and what is the measure of my days?
(Psalm 39:5)

Shefa Gold

MY CUP
כּוֹסִי רְוָיָה
Kosi r'vayah.
My cup overflows.
(Psalm 23:5)

Shefa Gold

CALLING FORTH THE HIDDEN POWER

קוּמָה יהוה הוֹשִׁיעֵנִי אֱלֹהַי

Kumah Adonai, hoshi'eini Elohai.
Rise up, YHVH; save me, my God.
(Psalm 3:8)

Shefa Gold

Ku - mah A - do - nai, ho - shi' - ei - ni E - lo - hai. Ku-

hai. Ku - mah A - do - nai, ho - shi' - ei - ni E - lo - hai. Ku-

mah A - do - nai, ho - shi' - ei - ni E - lo - hai.

PREPARATION FOR RECONNECTING

חָנֵּנִי יהוה כִּי אֻמְלַל אָנִי

Choneini Yah ki umlal ani.
Grace me, Yah, for I am withered [disconnected].
(Psalm 6:3)

Shefa Gold

Voice 1

Cho - nei - ni Yah___ ki um - lal___ a - ni. Cho - nei - ni Yah___ ki um - lal___ a - ni.

Voice 2

EVEN IN THE DARKNESS
זָרַח בַּחֹשֶׁךְ אוֹר לַיְשָׁרִים חַנּוּן וְרַחוּם וְצַדִּיק

Zarach bachoshech or lay'sharim, chanun v'rachum v'tzadik.
Even in the darkness a light shines for the upright, gracious, compassionate, and just.
(Psalm 112:4)

Round   Shefa Gold

GIVING MY "SELF" IN SERVICE
אָנָּה יהוה כִּי־אֲנִי עַבְדֶּךָ אֲנִי עַבְדְּךָ

Anah Yah ki ani avdecha; ani avd'cha.
Please, God, for I am your servant; I am your servant.
(Psalm 116:16)

Shefa Gold

SUPPORTED

סָמוּךְ לִבּוֹ לֹא יִירָא

Samuch libo lo yira.

סָמוּךְ לִבָּה לֹא תִּירָא

Samuch liba lo tira.

Heart supported, fearless.
(Psalm 112:8)

Shefa Gold

EFR—ENERGY FIELD RECHARGE

אֱלֹהִים יְחָנֵּנוּ וִיבָרְכֵנוּ יָאֵר פָּנָיו אִתָּנוּ סֶלָה

Elohim y'choneinu vivarcheinu ya'eir panav itanu selah.

God, grace us, bless us; may its light shine among us, selah.
(Psalm 67:2)

Shefa Gold

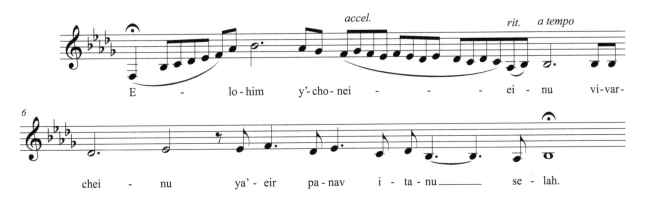

JUSTICE IN PEACE

יִפְרַח בְּיָמָיו צַדִּיק וְרֹב שָׁלוֹם

Yifrach b'yamav tzadik, v'rov shalom!
O justice, O justice ... in the fullness of peace!
O, justice shall flourish in its time, and the fullness of peace.
(Psalm 72:7)

Shefa Gold

RE-PARENTED

כִּי אָבִי וְאִמִּי עֲזָבוּנִי
וַיהוה יַאַסְפֵנִי
הוֹרֵנִי יהוה דַּרְכֶּךָ

Ki avi v'imi azavuni (2x)

V'Adonai ya'asfeini (4x)

Horeini Yah darkecha. (4x)

Though my father and my mother have forsaken me,
God will gather me in.
Teach me Your way, O God.
(Psalm 27:10–11)

Round   Shefa Gold

MORNING SONG

וַאֲנִי אָשִׁיר עֻזֶּךָ וַאֲרַנֵּן לַבֹּקֶר חַסְדֶּךָ

Va'ani ashir uzecha va'aranein labokeir chasdecha.
And I will sing Your glory and I will sing Your love in the morning.
(Psalm 59:17)

Shefa Gold

HEALING CHANT

מַה יָּקָר חַסְדְּךָ אֱלֹהִים

Mah yakar chasd'cha Elohim.

How precious is Your love, God.

(Psalm 36:8)

Shefa Gold

FROM THE DEPTHS

מִמַּעֲמַקִּים קְרָאתִיךָ יהוה

Mima'amakim k'raticha Yah!

From the depths I call to You, O God. Hear my voice!

(Psalm 130:1)

Shefa Gold

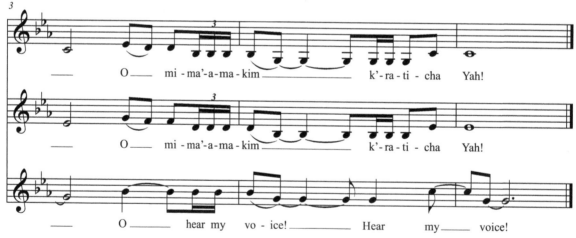

THE HEAVENS

הַשָּׁמַיִם מְסַפְּרִים כְּבוֹד־אֵל

Hashamayim m'saprim k'vod Eil.
The heavens open up and tell Your story,
of sun and clouds and storm, of wind and glory.
(Psalm 19:2)

Shefa Gold

RIVER OF BLISS
וְנַחַל עֲדָנֶיךָ תַשְׁקֵם

V'nachal adanecha tashkeim.
And from the river of Your bliss You will give them drink.

כִּי־עִמְּךָ מְקוֹר חַיִּים בְּאוֹרְךָ נִרְאֶה־אוֹר

Ki m'cha m'kor chayim; b'or'cha nireh or.
For with You is the source of life, in Your light we see light.

(Psalm 36:9–10)

Shefa Gold

Melody

V'na - chal a -da -ne -cha tash -keim. V'na -chal a -da -ne -cha tash - keim. V'na - keim.

Harmony

Ki__ im'- cha____ m'- kor cha -yim; __ b' - or'- cha ___ ni -reh or.____

For_ with You___ is the source of life, __ in __ Your light___ we see light._____

DAY AND NIGHT

יוֹם לְיוֹם יַבִּיעַ אֹמֶר וְלַיְלָה לְלַיְלָה יְחַוֶּה־דָּעַת

Yom l'yom yabia omer, v'lailah l'lailah y'chaveh da'at.

Day after day pours forth speech, night after night declares knowledge.

(Psalm 19:3)

ROSH HASHANAH CHANT

אַשְׁרֵי הָעָם יוֹדְעֵי תְרוּעָה יהוה בְּאוֹר־פָּנֶיךָ יְהַלֵּכוּן

Ashrei ha'am yodei t'ruah Adonai b'or panecha y'haleichun.

O God, happy are the people who know the blast of the shofar;
they walk in the light of Your presence.

(Psalm 89:16)

THE SEA LION'S QUESTION

מִי־הָאִישׁ הֶחָפֵץ חַיִּים אֹהֵב יָמִים לִרְאוֹת טוֹב

Mi ha'ish hechafeitz chayim, oheiv yamim lirot tov?
Who is the one that has a passion for life,
loving every day, seeing the good?
(Psalm 34:13)

Shefa Gold

PLANTING SEEDS OF JOY AND LIGHT

אוֹר זָרֻעַ לַצַּדִּיק וּלְיִשְׁרֵי לֵב שִׂמְחָה

Or zarua latzadik, ul'yishrei leiv simchah.

Plant the seeds of joy and light; tend them carefully day and night,
in this soil so dark and deep, I plant the dreams that love will reap.

(Psalm 97:11)

Shefa Gold

Or - za-ru-a___ la-tza-dik ul' - yish-rei leiv sim - chah. chah.

Plant the seeds of joy___ and light; tend them care-ful-ly day and night, in this soil so___

dark and deep, I plant the dreams___ that love will reap.

SINGING A NEW SONG

שִׁירוּ לַיהוה שִׁיר חָדָשׁ תְּהִלָּתוֹ בִּקְהַל חֲסִידִים

Halleluyah!
Shiru l'Adonai shir chadash; t'hilato bik'hal Chasidim.
Sing to God a new song;
God's praise is found in a community of lovers.
(Psalm 149:1)

Shefa Gold

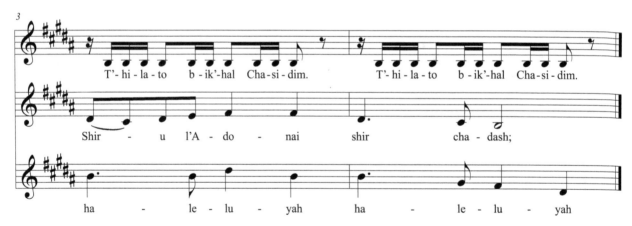

MIN HAMEITZAR

מִן־הַמֵּצַר קָרָאתִי יָהּ עָנָנִי בַמֶּרְחָב יָהּ

Min hameitzar karati Yah, anani vamerchav Yah.
From the narrow place I called out to God
who answered me with the divine expanse.
(Psalm 118:5)

Shefa Gold

SINGING GOD'S LOVE

חַסְדֵי יהוה עוֹלָם אָשִׁירָה

Chasdei Adonai olam ashirah.

I will sing forth from the hidden infinite, the loving-kindnesses of God.

(Psalm 89:1)

Shefa Gold

EXPANDING INNER SPACE

אֵלֶיךָ יהוה אֶקְרָא

Eilecha Yah ekra.

To You, God, I call.

(Psalm 30:9)

Shefa Gold

TUNING IN TO THE CREATOR-FUNCTION

אֶשָּׂא עֵינַי אֶל־הֶהָרִים מֵאַיִן יָבֹא עֶזְרִי

Esa einai el heharim mei'ayin yavo ezri. (2x)

My help comes from the One (3x)

Creator of heaven and earth.

(Psalm 12:11)

Round   Shefa Gold

E - sa ei -nai   el he - ha - rim mei'- a - yin ya - vo ez - ri.____

E - sa ei -nai   el he - ha - rim mei'- a - yin ya - vo ez - ri.____

My help comes from the One.   My help comes from the One.

My help comes from the One.   Cre - a - tor of hea - ven and earth.

PREPARATION FOR HEALING

אַתָּה עֻזִּי

אַתָּה חַיַּי

אַתָּה אוֹרִי

אַתָּה לְפָנַי

Atah Ozi

Atah Chayai

Atah Ori

Atah l'fanai

You are my Strength

You are my Life

You are my Light

Ever before me.

(inspired by Psalm 27)

Shefa Gold

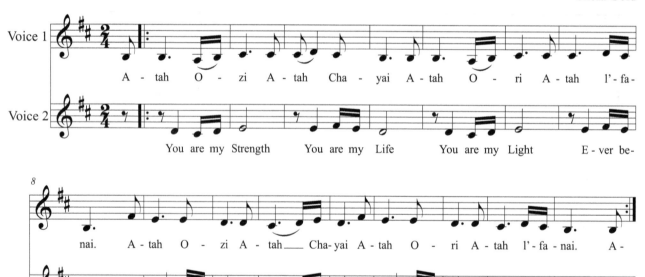

SOUL PERSPECTIVE
אֵלֶיךָ יהוה נַפְשִׁי אֶשָּׂא

Eilecha Yah nafshi esa.
To You, God, I lift up my soul.
(Psalm 25:1)

Shefa Gold

ENCOUNTERING THE LIVING GOD

צָמְאָה נַפְשִׁי לֵאלֹהִים לְאֵל חָי

Tzam'ah nafshi l'Eilohim l'Eil Chai.

My soul thirsts for God, for the Living God.

(Psalm 42:3)

Round

Shefa Gold

TURNING

סוּר מֵרָע וַעֲשֵׂה־טוֹב בַּקֵּשׁ שָׁלוֹם וְרָדְפֵהוּ

Sur meira va'asei tov, bakeish shalom v'radfeihu.

Turn away from evil and do good;
Seek peace/wholeness and go after it.

(Psalm 34:15)

Shefa Gold

SATISFACTION AND ITS FRUITS

שַׂבְּעֵנוּ בַבֹּקֶר חַסְדֶּךָ וּנְרַנְּנָה וְנִשְׂמְחָה בְּכָל־יָמֵינוּ

Sab'einu vaboker chasdecha;
Un'ran'nah v'nism'chah b'chol yameinu.
May Your loving-kindness satisfy us in the morning;
and we will sing out and we will rejoice for all our days.
(Psalm 90:14)

Shefa Gold

LONGING

כֵּן נַפְשִׁי תַעֲרֹג אֵלֶיךָ אֱלֹהִים

Kein nafshi ta'arog eilecha Elohim.

Just as the deer longs for water by the riverbank, so does my soul long for You, O God.

(Psalm 42:2)

Shefa Gold

TRUSTING

שַׁבְתִּי בְּבֵית־יהוה

Shavti b'veit Adonai.

I place myself in Your care.

(Psalm 23:6)

Shefa Gold

LET MY GLORY SING

יְזַמֶּרְךָ כָבוֹד וְלֹא יִדֹּם

Y'zamercha chavod v'lo yidom.
Let my glory sing to You and not be silenced.
(Psalm 30:13)

Shefa Gold

RE-MEMBERING

לַיהוה הָאָרֶץ וּמְלוֹאָהּ תֵּבֵל וְיֹשְׁבֵי בָהּ

L'Adonai ha'aretz um'loah, teiveil v'yosh'vei vah.

The earth and all that fills her, and all who dwell in her ... all belong to God.

(Psalm 24:1)

Shefa Gold

Melody

L'A - do - nai __ ha' - a - retz um' - lo - ah um' - lo - ah - lo - ah, tei - veil v'-yosh'-vei vah tei - veil v'-yosh'-vei vah tei - vah.

Harmony

HEART WALK

אֶתְהַלֵּךְ בְּתָם־לְבָבִי בְּקֶרֶב בֵּיתִי

Et'haleich b'tom l'vavi, b'kerev beiti.
I will walk within my house in the integrity of my heart.
(Psalm 101:2)

Shefa Gold

PROTECTING OUR "INNER CHILD"

כִּי־חִזַּק בְּרִיחֵי שְׁעָרָיִךְ בֵּרַךְ בָּנַיִךְ בְּקִרְבֵּךְ

Ki chizak b'richei sh'arayich, beirach banayich b'kirbeich.
When your boundaries are strong, your inner child is blessed.
(Psalm 147:13)

Shefa Gold

WHOSE FACE?

אַל־תַּסְתֵּר פָּנֶיךָ מִמֶּנִּי

Al tasteir panecha mimeni.
Do not hide Your face from me.
(Psalm 27:9)

3 part round

Shefa Gold

WITH EVERY BREATH

כֹּל הַנְּשָׁמָה תְּהַלֵּל יָהּ הַלְלוּיָהּ

Kol han'shamah t'haleil Yah.
Every soul praises Yah with every breath,
From the moment of birth until death! *Halleluyah!*
(Psalm 150:6)

Shefa Gold

PURE HEART
לֵב טָהוֹר בְּרָא־לִי אֱלֹהִים

Leiv tahor b'ra li Elohim.
Create for me a pure heart. [God] has created for me a pure heart.
O pure heart, create for me [the experience of] God.
The pure heart has created God for me.
(Psalm 51:12)

Shefa Gold

MY ROCK AND REDEEMER
אַתָּה צוּרִי וְגֹאֲלִי

Atah Tzuri v'Go'ali.
You are my Rock and my Redeemer.
(adapted from Psalm 19:15)

Shefa Gold

A SPIRIT OF "YES!"

וְרוּחַ נָכוֹן חַדֵּשׁ בְּקִרְבִּי

V'ruach nachon chadeish b'kirbi.

Renew within me a spirit of "Yes!"

(Psalm 51:12)

Shefa Gold

THE VALLEY OF DEATH

גַּם כִּי־אֵלֵךְ בְּגֵיא צַלְמָוֶת לֹא־אִירָא רָע

Gam ki eileich b'gei tzalmavet, lo ira ra.
Though I walk through the Valley of Death, I will not fear,
Though I walk through the Valley of Death, my God is near.
(Psalm 23:4)

Shefa Gold

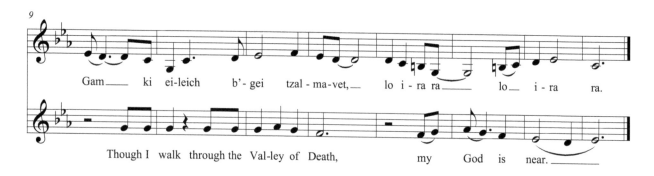

PURE

כָּל־מִשְׁבָּרֶיךָ וְגַלֶּיךָ עָלַי עָבָרוּ
טָהוֹר הוּא, טְהוֹרָה הִיא

Kol mishbarecha v'galecha alai avaru
Tahor hu, t'horah hi.
All of Your breakers and Your waves have swept over me.
He is pure; she is pure.
(Psalm 42:8)

Shefa Gold

MY PROTECTION
מָגִנִּי עַל־אֱלֹהִים מוֹשִׁיעַ יִשְׁרֵי־לֵב

Magini al Elohim, moshia yishrei leiv.
My protection is all about the God-field;
that's what saves the upright heart.
(Psalm 7:11)

Shefa Gold

WAITING ...
דּוֹם לַיהוה וְהִתְחוֹלֵל לוֹ

Dom l'Yah v'hitcholeil lo.
Be still and wait for God.
(Psalm 37:7)

Shefa Gold

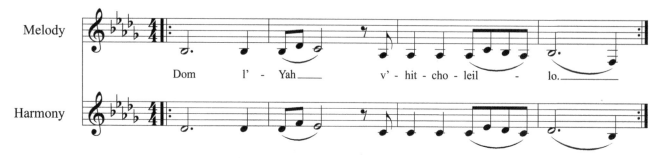

MY PRAYER AS INCENSE

תִּכּוֹן תְּפִלָּתִי קְטֹרֶת לְפָנֶיךָ

Tikon t'filati k'toret l'fanecha.

Let my prayer be incense before You.

(Psalm 141:2)

Shefa Gold

FROM WORLD TO WORLD

מֵעוֹלָם עַד־עוֹלָם אַתָּה אֵל

Mei'olam ad olam atah Eil.

From world to world, You are God.

(Psalm 90:2)

Shefa Gold

ALWAYS WITH YOU

וַאֲנִי תָמִיד עִמָּךְ

Va'ani tamid imach.
I am always with You.
Though my heart is troubled and I'm filled with dread
I turn to face Your Mystery
Though I've been lost inside my head
I open to Eternity.
(Psalm 73:23)

Shefa Gold

THE DAILY
PSALMS

FROM THE PSALM FOR SUNDAY

Psalm 24:9

שְׂאוּ שְׁעָרִים רָאשֵׁיכֶם וּשְׂאוּ פִּתְחֵי עוֹלָם

S'u sh'arim rasheichem, us'u pitchei olam!

Lift up your head, O you gates; lift them up, you everlasting doors!

Round

Shefa Gold

S' - u   sh' - a - rim   ra-shei - chem,   u - s'-

u ____ pit-chei   o - lam! ____   S' - u   sh' - a - rim   ra-shei -

chem,   u - s' - u ____   pit - chei   o - lam! ____   S'-

FROM THE PSALM FOR MONDAY

Psalm 48:10

דִּמִּינוּ אֱלֹהִים חַסְדֶּךָ

Diminu Elohim chasdecha.
Our stillness/silence is Your love, God.

Shefa Gold

FROM THE PSALM FOR TUESDAY

Psalm 82:8

קוּמָה אֱלֹהִים שָׁפְטָה הָאָרֶץ

Kumah Elohim shaftah ha'aretz.
Arise, God, and judge the land.

Shefa Gold

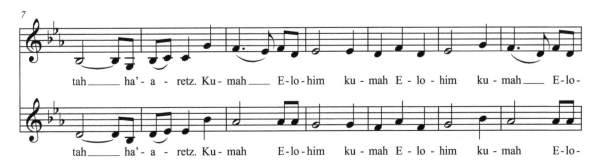

FROM THE PSALM FOR WEDNESDAY

Psalm 94:19

בְּרֹב שַׂרְעַפַּי בְּקִרְבִּי תַּנְחוּמֶיךָ יְשַׁעַשְׁעוּ נַפְשִׁי

B'rov sarapai b'kirbi,

Tanchumecha y'sha'ashu nafshi.

When worries multiply within me, Your comfort soothes my soul.

Shefa Gold

FROM THE PSALM FOR THURSDAY

Psalm 81:4–5

תִּקְעוּ בַחֹדֶשׁ שׁוֹפָר בַּכֶּסֶה לְיוֹם חַגֵּנוּ

כִּי חֹק לְיִשְׂרָאֵל הוּא מִשְׁפָּט לֵאלֹהֵי יַעֲקֹב

Tiku vachodesh shofar

Ba'keiseh l'yom chageinu

Ki chok l'Yisrael hu mishpat Elohei Ya'akov.

Sound a shofar at the new moon ... at the moment of concealment/potential for our celebration day.

It is a statute for Israel; it is a rule for Jacob.

Shefa Gold

FROM THE PSALM FOR FRIDAY

Psalm 93:2

נָכוֹן כִּסְאֲךָ מֵאָז מֵעוֹלָם אָתָּה

Nachon kisacha mei'az, mei'olam atah!

Your throne was long ago secured; beyond eternity are You!

Shefa Gold

FROM THE PSALM FOR SHABBAT

Psalm 92:6

מַה־גָּדְלוּ מַעֲשֶׂיךָ יהוה מְאֹד עָמְקוּ מַחְשְׁבֹתֶיךָ

Mah gadlu ma'asecha Yah, m'od am'ku machsh'votecha!

How great is Your work, O God, how very deep are Your thoughts!

Shefa Gold

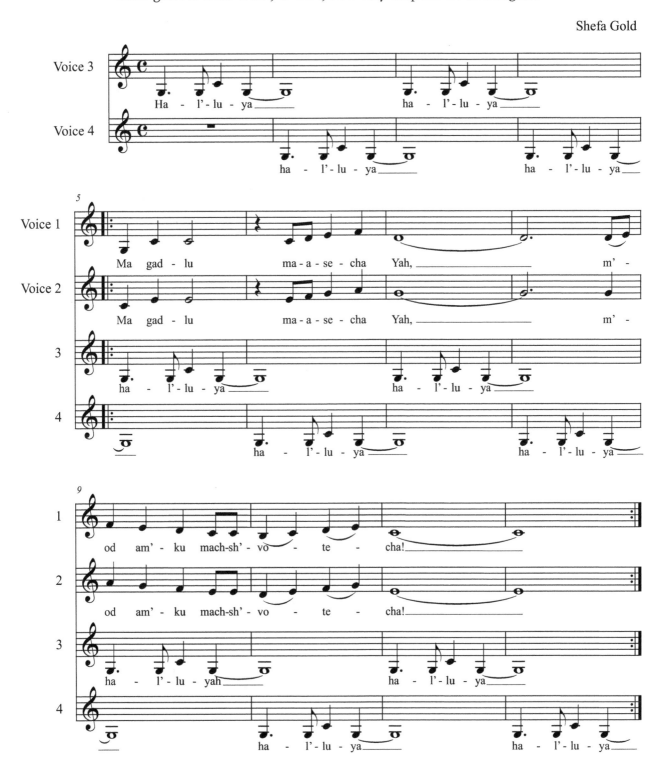

ISAIAH

THE MIRACLE

וַיָּשֶׂם מִדְבָּרָה כְּעֵדֶן וְעַרְבָתָה כְּגַן־יהוה

Vayasem midbarah k'eiden, v'arvatah k'gan Adonai.
He transforms her wilderness into delight,
her wasteland into a divine garden.
(Isaiah 51:3)

Shefa Gold

DIVINE CONGRATULATIONS

כִּי מָלְאָה צְבָאָהּ

Ki malah tz'va'ah.
Her time of service is fulfilled.
(Isaiah 40:2)

(Add parts one at a time)

Shefa Gold

AWAKENING THE HEART

הִתְעוֹרְרִי הִתְעוֹרְרִי קוּמִי יְרוּשָׁלַיִם

Hitor'ri, hitor'ri, kumi Y'rushalayim!
Awake, awake, arise Jerusalem!
(Isaiah 51:17)

Shefa Gold

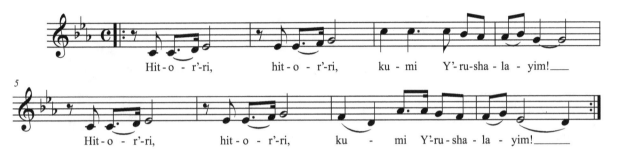

Hit - o - r'-ri, hit - o - r'-ri, ku - mi Y'-ru-sha - la - yim!____

Hit - o - r'-ri, hit - o - r'-ri, ku - mi Y'-ru-sha - la - yim!____

BREAKTHROUGH

עִבְרוּ עִבְרוּ בַּשְּׁעָרִים פַּנּוּ דֶּרֶךְ הָעָם

Ivru, ivru bash'arim, panu derech ha'am!
Go through, go through the gates, clear the way of the people!
(Isaiah 62:10)

Shefa Gold

Melody

Iv - ru, iv - ru ba-sh'-a - rim, pa - nu de - rech ha'-am!____

Harmony

Iv - ru, iv - ru ba-sh'-a - rim, pa - nu de - rech ha'-am!

COME FOR WATER!
הוֹי כָּל־צָמֵא לְכוּ לַמַּיִם

Hoy! Kol tzamei l'chu lamayim!
All who are thirsty, come for water!
(Isaiah 55:1)

Round   Shefa Gold

Hoy! Kol tza - mei_____ Hoy! Kol tza - mei Hoy! Kol tza - mei_____
Hoy! Kol tza - mei l' chu la - ma - a - yim l'-chu la - ma - a - yim l'-
chu la - ma - a - yim l' - chu la - ma - a - yim!

GETTING PERSPECTIVE
עַל הַר־גָּבֹהַּ עֲלִי־לָךְ

Al har gavo'ah ali lach.
Get yourself up upon the high mountain.
(Isaiah 40:9)

Double Round   Shefa Gold

Round #1

Al__ har ga-vo' - ah a - li__ lach.__ Al har ga-vo' - ah a - li__ lach.__

Round #2

Al har ga-vo' - ah a - li_____ lach. Al har ga-vo' - ah a - li_____ lach.

PALMISTRY

הֵן עַל־כַּפַּיִם חַקֹּתִיךְ

Hein al kapayim chakotich.

You are engraved on the palm of My hand.

(Isaiah 49:16)

Tango

Shefa Gold

SHINING

קוּמִי אוֹרִי כִּי־בָא אוֹרֵךְ וּכְבוֹד יהוה עָלַיִךְ זָרָח

Kumi ori ki va oreich uch'vod Adonai alayich zarach.
Arise and shine for your light has come,
and the Glory of God is shining upon you.
(Isaiah 60:1)

Shefa Gold

FOR IN JOY

כִּי־בְשִׂמְחָה תֵצֵאוּ וּבְשָׁלוֹם תּוּבָלוּן

Ki v'simchah teitzei'u, uv'shalom tuvalun.
For in joy will you go out, in peace be led across the Land,
Mountains and hills will burst into song,
And the trees of the field will clap their hands. (Clap!)
(Isaiah 55:12)

Shefa Gold

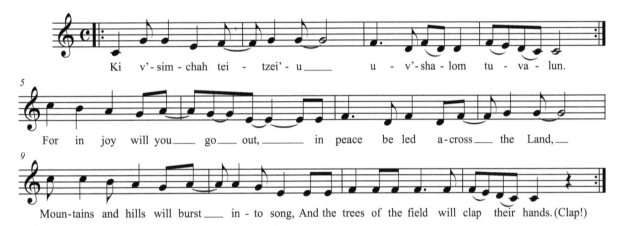

DELIGHT

אָז תִּתְעַנַּג עַל־יהוה

Az titanag al Havayah.
Then you will delight in God (being itself!)
(Isaiah 58:14)

Shefa Gold

SPACIOUSNESS

הַרְחִיבִי מְקוֹם אָהֳלֵךְ

Harchivi m'kom ohaleich.

Enlarge the place of your tent.

(Isaiah 54:2)

Note values are approximate. Sing freely.

Shefa Gold

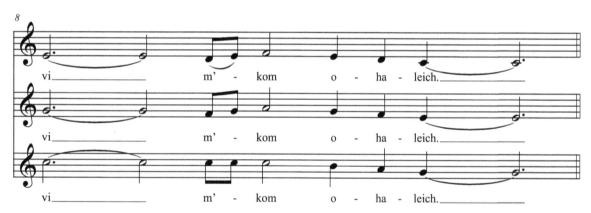

PEACE LIKE A RIVER

הִנְנִי נֹטֶה־אֵלֶיהָ כְּנָהָר שָׁלוֹם

Hin'ni, noteh eileha k'nahar shalom.

Here I am, extending peace to her like a river.

(Isaiah 66:12)

Shefa Gold

HERALDS OF PEACE

מַה־נָּאווּ עַל־הֶהָרִים רַגְלֵי מְבַשֵּׂר מַשְׁמִיעַ שָׁלוֹם

Mah navu al heharim raglei m'vaseir mashmia shalom.

Oh, how lovely—our footsteps on the mountain; we are messengers; we are heralds of peace.

(Isaiah 52:7)

Shefa Gold

COMFORT

נַחֲמוּ נַחֲמוּ עַמִּי

Nachamu, nachamu ami!

Comfort, comfort my people!

(Isaiah 40:1)

Shefa Gold

THROUGH THE WATERS

כִּי־תַעֲבֹר בַּמַּיִם אִתְּךָ־אָנִי וּבַנְּהָרוֹת לֹא יִשְׁטְפוּךָ

Ki ta'avor bamayim it'cha ani, uvan'harot lo yisht'fucha.
When you pass through the waters, I am with you, yes, I am with you.
I won't let the rivers overwhelm you, I will be with you.
(Isaiah 43:2)

Shefa Gold

GARMENTS OF SALVATION

שׂוֹשׂ אָשִׂישׂ בַּיהוה תָּגֵל נַפְשִׁי בֵּאלֹהַי
כִּי הִלְבִּישַׁנִי בִּגְדֵי־יֶשַׁע

Sos asis badonai tageil nafshi beilohai,

ki hilbishani bigdei yesha.

I will rejoice in God, who has dressed me in the garments of salvation.

(Isaiah 61:10)

Round   Shefa Gold

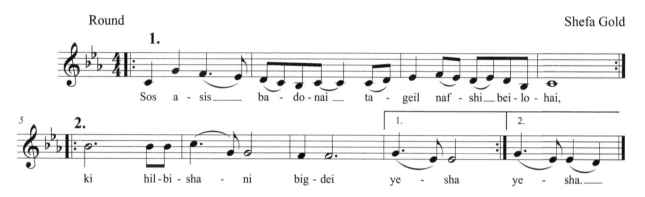

SEND ME!

אֶת־מִי אֶשְׁלַח וּמִי יֵלֶךְ־לָנוּ
הִנְנִי שְׁלָחֵנִי

Et mi eshlach umi yeilech lanu?

Hin'ni sh'lacheini.

Whom shall I send, and who shall go for us?

Here I am. Send me.

(Isaiah 6:8)

Shefa Gold

Form: Part 1 alone (with repeat), Part 2 (with repeat), Part 1 (with repeat), thereafter both parts together

MINDFULNESS
שִׁמְעוּ שָׁמוֹעַ אֵלַי וְאִכְלוּ־טוֹב

Shim'u shamo'a eilai, v'ichlu tov.
If you really listen to Me, then you will eat what is good.
(And your souls will delight in richness.)
(Isaiah 55:2)

Index of First Lines

Bible Study / Midrash

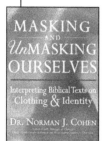

The Book of Job: Annotated & Explained
Translation and Annotation by Donald Kraus; Foreword by Dr. Marc Brettler
Clarifies for today's readers what Job is, how to overcome difficulties in the text, and what it may mean for us. Features fresh translation and probing commentary.
5½ x 8½, 256 pp, Quality PB, 978-1-59473-389-5 **$16.99**

Masking and Unmasking Ourselves: Interpreting Biblical Texts on Clothing & Identity *By Dr. Norman J. Cohen*
Presents ten Bible stories that involve clothing in an essential way, as a means of learning about the text, its characters and their interactions.
6 x 9, 240 pp, HC, 978-1-58023-461-0 **$24.99**

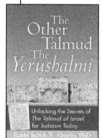

The Other Talmud—*The Yerushalmi*: Unlocking the Secrets of The Talmud of Israel for Judaism Today *By Rabbi Judith Z. Abrams, PhD*
A fascinating—and stimulating—look at "the other Talmud" and the possibilities for Jewish life reflected there.   6 x 9, 256 pp, HC, 978-1-58023-463-4 **$24.99**

The Torah Revolution: Fourteen Truths That Changed the World
By Rabbi Reuven Hammer, PhD   A unique look at the Torah and the revolutionary teachings of Moses embedded within it that gave birth to Judaism and influenced the world.   6 x 9, 240 pp, HC, 978-1-58023-457-3 **$24.99**

Ecclesiastes: Annotated & Explained
Translation and Annotation by Rabbi Rami Shapiro; Foreword by Rev. Barbara Cawthorne Crafton
5½ x 8½, 160 pp, Quality PB, 978-1-59473-287-4 **$16.99**

Ethics of the Sages: *Pirke Avot*—Annotated & Explained   *Translation and Annotation by Rabbi Rami Shapiro* 5½ x 8½, 192 pp, Quality PB, 978-1-59473-207-2 **$16.99**

The Genesis of Leadership: What the Bible Teaches Us about Vision, Values and Leading Change *By Rabbi Nathan Laufer; Foreword by Senator Joseph I. Lieberman*
6 x 9, 288 pp, Quality PB, 978-1-58023-352-1 **$18.99**

Hineini in Our Lives: Learning How to Respond to Others through 14 Biblical Texts and Personal Stories *By Rabbi Norman J. Cohen, PhD* 6 x 9, 240 pp, Quality PB, 978-1-58023-274-6 **$16.99**

A Man's Responsibility: A Jewish Guide to Being a Son, a Partner in Marriage, a Father and a Community Leader *By Rabbi Joseph B. Meszler* 6 x 9, 192 pp, Quality PB, 978-1-58023-435-1 **$16.99**

The Modern Men's Torah Commentary: New Insights from Jewish Men on the 54 Weekly Torah Portions *Edited by Rabbi Jeffrey K. Salkin*
6 x 9, 368 pp, HC, 978-1-58023-395-8 **$24.99**

Moses and the Journey to Leadership: Timeless Lessons of Effective Management from the Bible and Today's Leaders *By Rabbi Norman J. Cohen, PhD*
6 x 9, 240 pp, Quality PB, 978-1-58023-351-4 **$18.99**; HC, 978-1-58023-227-2 **$21.99**

Proverbs: Annotated & Explained
Translation and Annotation by Rabbi Rami Shapiro
5½ x 8½, 288 pp, Quality PB, 978-1-59473-310-9 **$16.99**

Righteous Gentiles in the Hebrew Bible: Ancient Role Models for Sacred Relationships
By Rabbi Jeffrey K. Salkin; Foreword by Rabbi Harold M. Schulweis;
Preface by Phyllis Tickle 6 x 9, 192 pp, Quality PB, 978-1-58023-364-4 **$18.99**

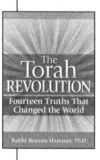

Sage Tales: Wisdom and Wonder from the Rabbis of the Talmud
By Rabbi Burton L. Visotzky 6 x 9, 256 pp, HC, 978-1-58023-456-6 **$24.99**

The Wisdom of Judaism: An Introduction to the Values of the Talmud
By Rabbi Dov Peretz Elkins 6 x 9, 192 pp, Quality PB, 978-1-58023-327-9 **$16.99**

Congregation Resources

Jewish Megatrends: Charting the Course of the American Jewish Future
By Rabbi Sidney Schwarz; Foreword by Ambassador Stuart E. Eizenstat
Visionary solutions for a community ripe for transformational change—from fourteen leading innovators of Jewish life.
6 x 9, 288 pp, HC, 978-1-58023-667-6 **$24.99**

Relational Judaism: Using the Power of Relationships to Transform the Jewish Community *By Dr. Ron Wolfson*
How to transform the model of twentieth-century Jewish institutions into twenty-first-century relational communities offering meaning and purpose, belonging and blessing.
6 x 9, 288 pp, HC, 978-1-58023-666-9 **$24.99**

Revolution of Jewish Spirit: How to Revive *Ruakh* in Your Spiritual Life, Transform Your Synagogue & Inspire Your Jewish Community
By Rabbi Baruch HaLevi, DMin, and Ellen Frankel, LCSW; Foreword by Dr. Ron Wolfson
A practical and engaging guide to reinvigorating Jewish life. Offers strategies for sustaining and expanding transformation, impassioned leadership, inspired programming and inviting sacred spaces.
6 x 9, 224 pp, Quality PB Original, 978-1-58023-625-6 **$19.99**

Building a Successful Volunteer Culture: Finding Meaning in Service in the Jewish Community *By Rabbi Charles Simon; Foreword by Shelley Lindauer; Preface by Dr. Ron Wolfson*
6 x 9, 192 pp, Quality PB, 978-1-58023-408-5 **$16.99**

The Case for Jewish Peoplehood: Can We Be One?
By Dr. Erica Brown and Dr. Misha Galperin; Foreword by Rabbi Joseph Telushkin
6 x 9, 224 pp, HC, 978-1-58023-401-6 **$21.99**

Empowered Judaism: What Independent Minyanim Can Teach Us about Building Vibrant Jewish Communities *By Rabbi Elie Kaunfer; Foreword by Prof. Jonathan D. Sarna*
6 x 9, 224 pp, Quality PB, 978-1-58023-412-2 **$18.99**

Finding a Spiritual Home: How a New Generation of Jews Can Transform the American Synagogue *By Rabbi Sidney Schwarz*
6 x 9, 352 pp, Quality PB, 978-1-58023-185-5 **$19.95**

Inspired Jewish Leadership: Practical Approaches to Building Strong Communities
By Dr. Erica Brown 6 x 9, 256 pp, HC, 978-1-58023-361-3 **$27.99**

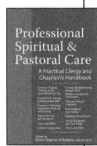

Jewish Pastoral Care, 2nd Edition: A Practical Handbook from Traditional & Contemporary Sources *Edited by Rabbi Dayle A. Friedman, MSW, MAJCS, BCC*
6 x 9, 528 pp, Quality PB, 978-1-58023-427-6 **$35.00**

Jewish Spiritual Direction: An Innovative Guide from Traditional and Contemporary Sources
Edited by Rabbi Howard A. Addison, PhD, and Barbara Eve Breitman, MSW
6 x 9, 368 pp, HC, 978-1-58023-230-2 **$30.00**

A Practical Guide to Rabbinic Counseling
Edited by Rabbi Yisrael N. Levitz, PhD, and Rabbi Abraham J. Twerski, MD
6 x 9, 432 pp, HC, 978-1-58023-562-4 **$40.00**

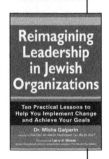

Professional Spiritual & Pastoral Care: A Practical Clergy and Chaplain's Handbook
Edited by Rabbi Stephen B. Roberts, MBA, MHL, BCJC
6 x 9, 480 pp, HC, 978-1-59473-312-3 **$50.00**

Reimagining Leadership in Jewish Organizations: Ten Practical Lessons to Help You Implement Change and Achieve Your Goals *By Dr. Misha Galperin*
6 x 9, 192 pp, Quality PB, 978-1-58023-492-4 **$16.99**

Rethinking Synagogues: A New Vocabulary for Congregational Life
By Rabbi Lawrence A. Hoffman, PhD 6 x 9, 240 pp, Quality PB, 978-1-58023-248-7 **$19.99**

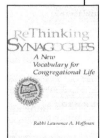

Spiritual Community: The Power to Restore Hope, Commitment and Joy
By Rabbi David A. Teutsch, PhD
5½ x 8½, 144 pp, HC, 978-1-58023-270-8 **$19.99**

Spiritual Boredom: Rediscovering the Wonder of Judaism *By Dr. Erica Brown*
6 x 9, 208 pp, HC, 978-1-58023-405-4 **$21.99**

The Spirituality of Welcoming: How to Transform Your Congregation into a Sacred Community *By Dr. Ron Wolfson* 6 x 9, 224 pp, Quality PB, 978-1-58023-244-9 **$19.99**

Bar / Bat Mitzvah

The Mitzvah Project Book
Making Mitzvah Part of Your Bar/Bat Mitzvah ... and Your Life
By Liz Suneby and Diane Heiman; Foreword by Rabbi Jeffrey K. Salkin; Preface by Rabbi Sharon Brous
The go-to source for Jewish young adults and their families looking to make the world a better place through good deeds—big or small.
6 x 9, 224 pp, Quality PB Original, 978-1-58023-458-0 **$16.99** For ages 11–13

The Bar/Bat Mitzvah Memory Book, 2nd Edition: An Album for Treasuring the Spiritual Celebration
By Rabbi Jeffrey K. Salkin and Nina Salkin
8 x 10, 48 pp, 2-color text, Deluxe HC, ribbon marker, 978-1-58023-263-0 **$19.99**

For Kids—Putting God on Your Guest List, 2nd Edition: How to Claim the Spiritual Meaning of Your Bar or Bat Mitzvah *By Rabbi Jeffrey K. Salkin*
6 x 9, 144 pp, Quality PB, 978-1-58023-308-8 **$15.99** For ages 11–13

The Jewish Prophet: Visionary Words from Moses and Miriam to Henrietta Szold and A. J. Heschel *By Rabbi Dr. Michael J. Shire*
6½ x 8½, 128 pp, 123 full-color illus., HC, 978-1-58023-168-8 **$14.95**

Putting God on the Guest List, 3rd Edition: How to Reclaim the Spiritual Meaning of Your Child's Bar or Bat Mitzvah *By Rabbi Jeffrey K. Salkin*
6 x 9, 224 pp, Quality PB, 978-1-58023-222-7 **$16.99**; HC, 978-1-58023-260-9 **$24.99**

Putting God on the Guest List Teacher's Guide
8½ x 11, 48 pp, PB, 978-1-58023-226-5 **$8.99**

Teens / Young Adults

Text Messages: A Torah Commentary for Teens
Edited by Rabbi Jeffrey K. Salkin
Shows today's teens how each Torah portion contains worlds of meaning for them, for what they are going through in their lives, and how they can shape their Jewish identity as they enter adulthood.
6 x 9, 304 pp (est), HC, 978-1-58023-507-5 **$24.99**

Hannah Senesh: Her Life and Diary, the First Complete Edition
By Hannah Senesh; Foreword by Marge Piercy; Preface by Eitan Senesh; Afterword by Roberta Grossman
6 x 9, 368 pp, b/w photos, Quality PB, 978-1-58023-342-2 **$19.99**

I Am Jewish: Personal Reflections Inspired by the Last Words of Daniel Pearl
Edited by Judea and Ruth Pearl 6 x 9, 304 pp, Deluxe PB w/ flaps, 978-1-58023-259-3 **$18.99**
Download a free copy of the *I Am Jewish Teacher's Guide* at www.jewishlights.com.

The JGirl's Guide: The Young Jewish Woman's Handbook for Coming of Age
By Penina Adelman, Ali Feldman and Shulamit Reinharz
6 x 9, 240 pp, Quality PB, 978-1-58023-215-9 **$14.99** For ages 11 & up

The JGirl's Teacher's and Parent's Guide
8½ x 11, 56 pp, PB, 978-1-58023-225-8 **$8.99**

Tough Questions Jews Ask, 2nd Edition: A Young Adult's Guide to Building a Jewish Life *By Rabbi Edward Feinstein*
6 x 9, 160 pp, Quality PB, 978-1-58023-454-2 **$16.99** For ages 11 & up

Tough Questions Jews Ask Teacher's Guide
8½ x 11, 72 pp, PB, 978-1-58023-187-9 **$8.95**

Pre-Teens

Be Like God: God's To-Do List for Kids
By Dr. Ron Wolfson
Encourages kids ages eight through twelve to use their God-given superpowers to find the many ways they can make a difference in the lives of others and find meaning and purpose for their own.
7 x 9, 144 pp, Quality PB, 978-1-58023-510-5 **$15.99** For ages 8–12

The Book of Miracles: A Young Person's Guide to Jewish Spiritual Awareness
By Lawrence Kushner, with all-new illustrations by the author.
6 x 9, 96 pp, 2-color illus., HC, 978-1-879045-78-1 **$16.95** For ages 9–13

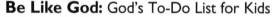

Children's Books

Around the World in One Shabbat
Jewish People Celebrate the Sabbath Together
By Durga Yael Bernhard
Takes your child on a colorful adventure to share the many ways Jewish people celebrate Shabbat around the world.
11 x 8½, 32 pp, Full-color illus., HC, 978-1-58023-433-7 **$18.99** *For ages 3–6*

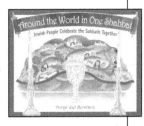

It's a ... It's a ... It's a Mitzvah
By Liz Suneby and Diane Heiman; Full-color Illus. by Laurel Molk
Join Mitzvah Meerkat and friends as they introduce children to the everyday kindnesses that mark the beginning of a Jewish journey and a lifetime commitment to *tikkun olam* (repairing the world).
9 x 12, 32 pp, Full-color illus., HC, 978-1-58023-509-9 **$18.99** *For ages 3–6*

What You Will See Inside a Synagogue
By Rabbi Lawrence A. Hoffman, PhD, and Dr. Ron Wolfson; Full-color photos by Bill Aron
A colorful, fun-to-read introduction that explains the ways and whys of Jewish worship and religious life.
8½ x 10½, 32 pp, Full-color photos, Quality PB, 978-1-59473-256-0 **$8.99** *For ages 6 & up*
(A book from SkyLight Paths, Jewish Lights' sister imprint)

Because Nothing Looks Like God
By Lawrence Kushner and Karen Kushner
Real-life examples of happiness and sadness—from goodnight stories, to the hope and fear felt the first time at bat, to the closing moments of someone's life—invite parents and children to explore, together, the questions we all have about God, no matter what our age. 11 x 8½, 32 pp, Full-color illus., HC, 978-1-58023-092-6 **$18.99** *For ages 4 & up*

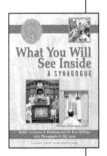

The Book of Miracles: A Young Person's Guide to Jewish Spiritual Awareness
Written and illus. by Lawrence Kushner
Easy-to-read, imaginatively illustrated book encourages kids' awareness of their own spirituality. Revealing the essence of Judaism in a language they can understand and enjoy. 6 x 9, 96 pp, 2-color illus., HC, 978-1-879045-78-1 **$16.95** *For ages 9–13*

In God's Hands   *By Lawrence Kushner and Gary Schmidt*
Brings new life to a traditional Jewish folktale, reminding parents and kids of all faiths and all backgrounds that each of us has the power to make the world a better place—working ordinary miracles with our everyday deeds.
9 x 12, 32 pp, Full-color illus., HC, 978-1-58023-224-1 **$16.99** *For ages 5 & up*

In Our Image: God's First Creatures
By Nancy Sohn Swartz
A playful new twist to the Genesis story, God asks all of nature to offer gifts to humankind—with a promise that the humans would care for creation in return.
9 x 12, 32 pp, Full-color illus., HC, 978-1-879045-99-6 **$16.95** *For ages 4 & up*

The Jewish Family Fun Book, 2nd Ed.
Holiday Projects, Everyday Activities, and Travel Ideas with Jewish Themes
By Danielle Dardashti and Roni Sarig
The complete sourcebook for families wanting to put a new spin on activities for Jewish holidays, holy days and the everyday. It offers dozens of easy-to-do activities that bring Jewish tradition to life for kids of all ages.
6 x 9, 304 pp, w/ 70+ b/w illus., Quality PB, 978-1-58023-333-0 **$18.99**

The Kids' Fun Book of Jewish Time   *By Emily Sper*
A unique way to introduce children to the Jewish calendar—night and day, the seven-day week, Shabbat, the Hebrew months, seasons and dates.
9 x 7½, 24 pp, Full-color illus., HC, 978-1-58023-311-8 **$16.99** *For ages 3–6*

What Makes Someone a Jew?   *By Lauren Seidman*
Reflects the changing face of American Judaism. Helps preschoolers and young readers (ages 3–6) understand that you don't have to look a certain way to be Jewish.
10 x 8½, 32 pp, Full-color photos, Quality PB, 978-1-58023-321-7 **$8.99** *For ages 3–6*

When a Grandparent Dies: A Kid's Own Remembering Workbook for Dealing with Shiva
and the Year Beyond   *By Nechama Liss-Levinson*
8 x 10, 48 pp, 2-color text, HC, 978-1-879045-44-6 **$15.95** *For ages 7–13*

Children's Books by Sandy Eisenberg Sasso

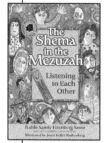

The *Shema* in the Mezuzah: Listening to Each Other
By Sandy Eisenberg Sasso; Full-color Illus. by Joani Keller Rothenberg
Introduces children ages 3 to 6 to the words of the *Shema* and the custom of putting up the mezuzah. Winner, National Jewish Book Award
9 x 12, 32 pp, Full-color illus., HC, 978-1-58023-506-8 **$18.99**

Adam & Eve's First Sunset: God's New Day
Explores fear and hope, faith and gratitude in ways that will delight kids and adults—inspiring us to bless each of God's days and nights.
9 x 12, 32 pp, Full-color illus., HC, 978-1-58023-177-0 **$17.95** *For ages 4 & up*

Also Available as a Board Book: Adam and Eve's New Day
5 x 5, 24 pp, Full-color illus., Board Book, 978-1-59473-205-8 **$7.99** *For ages 0–4*
(A book from SkyLight Paths, Jewish Lights' sister imprint)

But God Remembered: Stories of Women from Creation to the Promised Land
Four different stories of women—Lilith, Serach, Bityah and the Daughters of Z—teach us important values through their faith and actions.
9 x 12, 32 pp, Full-color illus., Quality PB, 978-1-58023-372-9 **$8.99** *For ages 8 & up*

For Heaven's Sake
Heaven is often found where you least expect it.
9 x 12, 32 pp, Full-color illus., HC, 978-1-58023-054-4 **$16.95** *For ages 4 & up*

God in Between
If you wanted to find God, where would you look? This magical, mythical tale teaches that God can be found where we are: within all of us and the relationships between us. 9 x 12, 32 pp, Full-color illus., HC, 978-1-879045-86-6 **$16.95** *For ages 4 & up*

God Said Amen
An inspiring story about hearing the answers to our prayers.
9 x 12, 32 pp, Full-color illus., HC, 978-1-58023-080-3 **$16.95** *For ages 4 & up*

God's Paintbrush: Special 10th Anniversary Edition
Wonderfully interactive, invites children of all faiths and backgrounds to encounter God through moments in their own lives. Provides questions adult and child can explore together. 11 x 8¼, 32 pp, Full-color illus., HC, 978-1-58023-195-4 **$17.95** *For ages 4 & up*

Also Available as a Board Book: I Am God's Paintbrush
5 x 5, 24 pp, Full-color illus., Board Book, 978-1-59473-265-2 **$7.99** *For ages 0–4*
(A book from SkyLight Paths, Jewish Lights' sister imprint)

Also Available: God's Paintbrush Teacher's Guide
8½ x 11, 32 pp, PB, 978-1-879045-57-6 **$8.95**

God's Paintbrush Celebration Kit
A Spiritual Activity Kit for Teachers and Students of All Faiths, All Backgrounds
9½ x 12, 40 Full-color Activity Sheets & Teacher Folder w/ complete instructions
HC, 978-1-58023-050-6 **$21.95**
8-Student Activity Sheet Pack (40 sheets/5 sessions), 978-1-58023-058-2 **$19.95**

In God's Name
Like an ancient myth in its poetic text and vibrant illustrations, this award-winning modern fable about the search for God's name celebrates the diversity and, at the same time, the unity of all people.
9 x 12, 32 pp, Full-color illus., HC, 978-1-879045-26-2 **$16.99** *For ages 4 & up*

Also Available as a Board Book: What Is God's Name?
5 x 5, 24 pp, Full-color illus., Board Book, 978-1-893361-10-2 **$7.99** *For ages 0–4*
(A book from SkyLight Paths, Jewish Lights' sister imprint)

Also Available in Spanish: El nombre de Dios
9 x 12, 32 pp, Full-color illus., HC, 978-1-893361-63-8 **$16.95** *For ages 4 & up*

Noah's Wife: The Story of Naamah
9 x 12, 32 pp, Full-color illus., HC, 978-1-58023-134-3 **$16.95** *For ages 4 & up*

Also Available as a Board Book: Naamah, Noah's Wife
5 x 5, 24 pp, Full-color illus., Board Book, 978-1-893361-56-0 **$7.95** *For ages 0–4*
(A book from SkyLight Paths, Jewish Lights' sister imprint)

Ecology / Environment

A Wild Faith: Jewish Ways into Wilderness, Wilderness Ways into Judaism
By Rabbi Mike Comins; Foreword by Nigel Savage 6 x 9, 240 pp, Quality PB, 978-1-58023-316-3 **$16.99**

Ecology & the Jewish Spirit: Where Nature & the Sacred Meet
Edited by Ellen Bernstein 6 x 9, 288 pp, Quality PB, 978-1-58023-082-7 **$18.99**

Torah of the Earth: Exploring 4,000 Years of Ecology in Jewish Thought
Vol. 1: Biblical Israel & Rabbinic Judaism; Vol. 2: Zionism & Eco-Judaism
Edited by Rabbi Arthur Waskow Vol. 1: 6 x 9, 272 pp, Quality PB, 978-1-58023-086-5 **$19.95**
Vol. 2: 6 x 9, 336 pp, Quality PB, 978-1-58023-087-2 **$19.95**

The Way Into Judaism and the Environment *By Jeremy Benstein, PhD*
6 x 9, 288 pp, Quality PB, 978-1-58023-368-2 **$18.99**; HC, 978-1-58023-268-5 **$24.99**

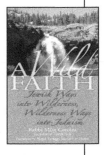

Graphic Novels / Graphic History

The Adventures of Rabbi Harvey: A Graphic Novel of Jewish Wisdom and Wit in the
Wild West *By Steve Sheinkin* 6 x 9, 144 pp, Full-color illus., Quality PB, 978-1-58023-310-1 **$16.99**

Rabbi Harvey Rides Again: A Graphic Novel of Jewish Folktales Let Loose in the
Wild West *By Steve Sheinkin* 6 x 9, 144 pp, Full-color illus., Quality PB, 978-1-58023-347-7 **$16.99**

Rabbi Harvey vs. the Wisdom Kid: A Graphic Novel of Dueling
Jewish Folktales in the Wild West *By Steve Sheinkin*
Rabbi Harvey's first book-length adventure—and toughest challenge.
6 x 9, 144 pp, Full-color illus., Quality PB, 978-1-58023-422-1 **$16.99**

The Story of the Jews: A 4,000-Year Adventure—A Graphic History Book
By Stan Mack 6 x 9, 288 pp, Illus., Quality PB, 978-1-58023-155-8 **$16.99**

Grief / Healing

Facing Illness, Finding God: How Judaism Can Help You and
Caregivers Cope When Body or Spirit Fails *By Rabbi Joseph B. Meszler*
Will help you find spiritual strength for healing amid the fear, pain and chaos of
illness. 6 x 9, 208 pp, Quality PB, 978-1-58023-423-8 **$16.99**

Midrash & Medicine: Healing Body and Soul in the Jewish Interpretive
Tradition *Edited by Rabbi William Cutter, PhD; Foreword by Michele F. Prince, LCSW, MAJCS*
Explores how midrash can help you see beyond the physical aspects of healing to
tune in to your spiritual source.
6 x 9, 352 pp, Quality PB, 978-1-58023-484-9 **$21.99**

Healing from Despair: Choosing Wholeness in a Broken World
By Rabbi Elie Kaplan Spitz with Erica Shapiro Taylor; Foreword by Abraham J. Twerski, MD
5½ x 8½, 208 pp, Quality PB, 978-1-58023-436-8 **$16.99**

Healing and the Jewish Imagination: Spiritual and Practical Perspectives on
Judaism and Health *Edited by Rabbi William Cutter, PhD*
6 x 9, 240 pp, Quality PB, 978-1-58023-373-6 **$19.99**

Grief in Our Seasons: A Mourner's Kaddish Companion *By Rabbi Kerry M. Olitzky*
4½ x 6½, 448 pp, Quality PB, 978-1-879045-55-2 **$15.95**

Healing of Soul, Healing of Body: Spiritual Leaders Unfold the Strength & Solace
in Psalms *Edited by Rabbi Simkha Y. Weintraub, LCSW*
6 x 9, 128 pp, 2-color illus. text, Quality PB, 978-1-879045-31-6 **$16.99**

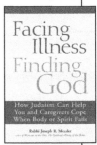

Mourning & Mitzvah, 2nd Edition: A Guided Journal for Walking the Mourner's
Path through Grief to Healing *By Rabbi Anne Brener, LCSW*
7½ x 9, 304 pp, Quality PB, 978-1-58023-113-8 **$19.99**

Tears of Sorrow, Seeds of Hope, 2nd Edition: A Jewish Spiritual Companion
for Infertility and Pregnancy Loss *By Rabbi Nina Beth Cardin*
6 x 9, 208 pp, Quality PB, 978-1-58023-233-3 **$18.99**

A Time to Mourn, a Time to Comfort, 2nd Edition: A Guide to Jewish
Bereavement *By Dr. Ron Wolfson; Foreword by Rabbi David J. Wolpe*
7 x 9, 384 pp, Quality PB, 978-1-58023-253-1 **$21.99**

When a Grandparent Dies: A Kid's Own Remembering Workbook for Dealing
with Shiva and the Year Beyond *By Nechama Liss-Levinson, PhD*
8 x 10, 48 pp, 2-color text, HC, 978-1-879045-44-6 **$15.95** *For ages 7–13*

Holidays / Holy Days

Prayers of Awe Series

An exciting new series that examines the High Holy Day liturgy to enrich the praying experience of everyone—whether experienced worshipers or guests who encounter Jewish prayer for the very first time.

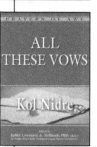

We Have Sinned—Sin and Confession in Judaism: Ashamnu and Al Chet
Edited by Rabbi Lawrence A. Hoffman, PhD
A varied and fascinating look at sin, confession and pardon in Judaism, as suggested by the centrality of *Ashamnu* and *Al Chet*, two prayers that people know so well, though understand so little.   6 x 9, 304 pp, HC, 978-1-58023-612-6 **$24.99**

Who by Fire, Who by Water—Un'taneh Tokef
Edited by Rabbi Lawrence A. Hoffman, PhD   6 x 9, 272 pp, HC, 978-1-58023-424-5 **$24.99**

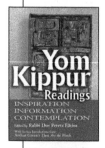

All These Vows—Kol Nidre
Edited by Rabbi Lawrence A. Hoffman, PhD   6 x 9, 288 pp, HC, 978-1-58023-430-6 **$24.99**

Rosh Hashanah Readings: Inspiration, Information and Contemplation
Yom Kippur Readings: Inspiration, Information and Contemplation
Edited by Rabbi Dov Peretz Elkins; Section Introductions from Arthur Green's These Are the Words
Rosh Hashanah: 6 x 9, 400 pp, Quality PB, 978-1-58023-437-5 **$19.99**
Yom Kippur: 6 x 9, 368 pp, Quality PB, 978-1-58023-438-2 **$19.99**; HC, 978-1-58023-271-5 **$24.99**

Reclaiming Judaism as a Spiritual Practice: Holy Days and Shabbat
By Rabbi Goldie Milgram   7 x 9, 272 pp, Quality PB, 978-1-58023-205-0 **$19.99**

The Sabbath Soul: Mystical Reflections on the Transformative Power of Holy Time
Selection, Translation and Commentary by Eitan Fishbane, PhD
6 x 9, 208 pp, Quality PB, 978-1-58023-459-7 **$18.99**

Shabbat, 2nd Edition: The Family Guide to Preparing for and Celebrating the Sabbath
By Dr. Ron Wolfson   7 x 9, 320 pp, Illus., Quality PB, 978-1-58023-164-0 **$19.99**

Hanukkah, 2nd Edition: The Family Guide to Spiritual Celebration
By Dr. Ron Wolfson   7 x 9, 240 pp, Illus., Quality PB, 978-1-58023-122-0 **$18.95**

Passover

My People's Passover Haggadah
Traditional Texts, Modern Commentaries
Edited by Rabbi Lawrence A. Hoffman, PhD, and David Arnow, PhD
A diverse and exciting collection of commentaries on the traditional Passover Haggadah—in two volumes!
Vol. 1: 7 x 10, 304 pp, HC, 978-1-58023-354-5 **$24.99**
Vol. 2: 7 x 10, 320 pp, HC, 978-1-58023-346-0 **$24.99**

Freedom Journeys: The Tale of Exodus and Wilderness across Millennia
By Rabbi Arthur O. Waskow and Rabbi Phyllis O. Berman
Explores how the story of Exodus echoes in our own time, calling us to relearn and rethink the Passover story through social-justice, ecological, feminist and interfaith perspectives.   6 x 9, 288 pp, HC, 978-1-58023-445-0 **$24.99**

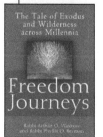

Leading the Passover Journey: The Seder's Meaning Revealed,
the Haggadah's Story Retold   *By Rabbi Nathan Laufer*
Uncovers the hidden meaning of the Seder's rituals and customs.
6 x 9, 224 pp, Quality PB, 978-1-58023-399-6 **$18.99**

Creating Lively Passover Seders, 2nd Edition: A Sourcebook of Engaging Tales,
Texts & Activities   *By David Arnow, PhD*   7 x 9, 464 pp, Quality PB, 978-1-58023-444-3 **$24.99**

Passover, 2nd Edition: The Family Guide to Spiritual Celebration
By Dr. Ron Wolfson with Joel Lurie Grishaver   7 x 9, 416 pp, Quality PB, 978-1-58023-174-9 **$19.95**

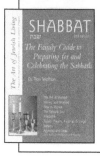

The Women's Passover Companion: Women's Reflections on the Festival of Freedom
Edited by Rabbi Sharon Cohen Anisfeld, Tara Mohr and Catherine Spector; Foreword by Paula E. Hyman
6 x 9, 352 pp, Quality PB, 978-1-58023-231-9 **$19.99**; HC, 978-1-58023-128-2 **$24.95**

The Women's Seder Sourcebook: Rituals & Readings for Use at the Passover Seder
Edited by Rabbi Sharon Cohen Anisfeld, Tara Mohr and Catherine Spector
6 x 9, 384 pp, Quality PB, 978-1-58023-232-6 **$19.99**

Life Cycle

Marriage / Parenting / Family / Aging

The New Jewish Baby Album: Creating and Celebrating the Beginning of a Spiritual Life—A Jewish Lights Companion
By the Editors at Jewish Lights; Foreword by Anita Diamant; Preface by Rabbi Sandy Eisenberg Sasso
A spiritual keepsake that will be treasured for generations. More than just a memory book, *shows you how—and why it's important*—to create a Jewish home and a Jewish life. 8 x 10, 64 pp, Deluxe Padded HC, Full-color illus., 978-1-58023-138-1 **$19.95**

The Jewish Pregnancy Book: A Resource for the Soul, Body & Mind during Pregnancy, Birth & the First Three Months *By Sandy Falk, MD, and Rabbi Daniel Judson, with Steven A. Rapp* Medical information, prayers and rituals for each stage of pregnancy. 7 x 10, 208 pp, b/w photos, Quality PB, 978-1-58023-178-7 **$16.95**

Celebrating Your New Jewish Daughter: Creating Jewish Ways to Welcome Baby Girls into the Covenant—New and Traditional Ceremonies *By Debra Nussbaum Cohen; Foreword by Rabbi Sandy Eisenberg Sasso* 6 x 9, 272 pp, Quality PB, 978-1-58023-090-2 **$18.95**

The New Jewish Baby Book, 2nd Edition: Names, Ceremonies & Customs—A Guide for Today's Families *By Anita Diamant* 6 x 9, 320 pp, Quality PB, 978-1-58023-251-7 **$19.99**

Parenting as a Spiritual Journey: Deepening Ordinary and Extraordinary Events into Sacred Occasions *By Rabbi Nancy Fuchs-Kreimer, PhD*
6 x 9, 224 pp, Quality PB, 978-1-58023-016-2 **$17.99**

Parenting Jewish Teens: A Guide for the Perplexed
By Joanne Doades Explores the questions and issues that shape the world in which today's Jewish teenagers live and offers constructive advice to parents.
6 x 9, 176 pp, Quality PB, 978-1-58023-305-7 **$16.99**

Judaism for Two: A Spiritual Guide for Strengthening and Celebrating Your Loving Relationship *By Rabbi Nancy Fuchs-Kreimer, PhD, and Rabbi Nancy H. Wiener, DMin; Foreword by Rabbi Elliot N. Dorff, PhD*
Addresses the ways Jewish teachings can enhance and strengthen committed relationships. 6 x 9, 224 pp, Quality PB, 978-1-58023-254-8 **$16.99**

The Creative Jewish Wedding Book, 2nd Edition: A Hands-On Guide to New & Old Traditions, Ceremonies & Celebrations *By Gabrielle Kaplan-Mayer*
9 x 9, 288 pp, b/w photos, Quality PB, 978-1-58023-398-9 **$19.99**

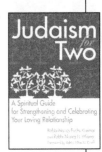

Divorce Is a Mitzvah: A Practical Guide to Finding Wholeness and Holiness When Your Marriage Dies *By Rabbi Perry Netter; Afterword by Rabbi Laura Geller*
6 x 9, 224 pp, Quality PB, 978-1-58023-172-5 **$16.95**

Embracing the Covenant: Converts to Judaism Talk About Why & How
By Rabbi Allan Berkowitz and Patti Moskovitz
6 x 9, 192 pp, Quality PB, 978-1-879045-50-7 **$16.95**

The Guide to Jewish Interfaith Family Life: An InterfaithFamily.com Handbook
Edited by Ronnie Friedland and Edmund Case
6 x 9, 384 pp, Quality PB, 978-1-58023-153-4 **$18.95**

A Heart of Wisdom: Making the Jewish Journey from Midlife through the Elder Years
Edited by Susan Berrin; Foreword by Rabbi Harold Kushner
6 x 9, 384 pp, Quality PB, 978-1-58023-051-3 **$18.95**

Introducing My Faith and My Community: The Jewish Outreach Institute Guide for the Christian in a Jewish Interfaith Relationship
By Rabbi Kerry M. Olitzky 6 x 9, 176 pp, Quality PB, 978-1-58023-192-3 **$16.99**

Making a Successful Jewish Interfaith Marriage: The Jewish Outreach Institute Guide to Opportunities, Challenges and Resources *By Rabbi Kerry M. Olitzky with Joan Peterson Littman*
6 x 9, 176 pp, Quality PB, 978-1-58023-170-1 **$16.95**

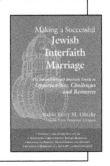

A Man's Responsibility: A Jewish Guide to Being a Son, a Partner in Marriage, a Father and a Community Leader *By Rabbi Joseph B. Meszler*
6 x 9, 192 pp, Quality PB, 978-1-58023-435-1 **$16.99**; HC, 978-1-58023-362-0 **$21.99**

So That Your Values Live On: Ethical Wills and How to Prepare Them
Edited by Rabbi Jack Riemer and Rabbi Nathaniel Stampfer
6 x 9, 272 pp, Quality PB, 978-1-879045-34-7 **$18.99**

Spirituality / Crafts

Jewish Threads: A Hands-On Guide to Stitching Spiritual Intention into Jewish Fabric Crafts *By Diana Drew with Robert Grayson*
Learn how to make your own Jewish fabric crafts with spiritual intention— a journey of creativity, imagination and inspiration. Thirty projects.
7 x 9, 288 pp, 8-page color insert, b/w illus., Quality PB Original, 978-1-58023-442-9 **$19.99**

(from SkyLight Paths, Jewish Lights' sister imprint)

Beading—The Creative Spirit: Finding Your Sacred Center through the Art of Beadwork *By Wendy Ellsworth*
Invites you on a spiritual pilgrimage into the kaleidoscope world of glass and color.
7 x 9, 240 pp, 8-page full-color insert, b/w photos and diagrams, Quality PB, 978-1-59473-267-6 **$18.99**

Contemplative Crochet: A Hands-On Guide for Interlocking Faith and Craft *By Cindy Crandall-Frazier; Foreword by Linda Skolnik*
Will take you on a path deeper into your crocheting and your spiritual awareness.
7 x 9, 208 pp, b/w photos, Quality PB, 978-1-59473-238-6 **$16.99**

The Knitting Way: A Guide to Spiritual Self-Discovery
By Linda Skolnik and Janice MacDaniels
Shows how to use knitting to strengthen your spiritual self.
7 x 9, 240 pp, b/w photos, Quality PB, 978-1-59473-079-5 **$16.99**

The Painting Path: Embodying Spiritual Discovery through Yoga, Brush and Color *By Linda Novick; Foreword by Richard Segalman*
Explores the divine connection you can experience through art.
7 x 9, 208 pp, 8-page full-color insert, b/w photos, Quality PB, 978-1-59473-226-3 **$18.99**

The Quilting Path: A Guide to Spiritual Self-Discovery through Fabric, Thread and Kabbalah *By Louise Silk* Explores how to cultivate personal growth through quilt making. 7 x 9, 192 pp, b/w photos, Quality PB, 978-1-59473-206-5 **$16.99**

The Scrapbooking Journey: A Hands-On Guide to Spiritual Discovery
By Cory Richardson-Lauve; Foreword by Stacy Julian
Reveals how this craft can become a practice used to deepen and shape your life.
7 x 9, 176 pp, 8-page full-color insert, b/w photos, Quality PB, 978-1-59473-216-4 **$18.99**

Travel

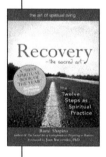

Israel—A Spiritual Travel Guide, 2nd Edition: A Companion for the Modern Jewish Pilgrim *By Rabbi Lawrence A. Hoffman, PhD*
Helps today's pilgrim tap into the deep spiritual meaning of the ancient—and modern—sites of the Holy Land.
4¾ x 10, 256 pp, Illus., Quality PB, 978-1-58023-261-6 **$18.99**

Also Available: **The Israel Mission Leader's Guide**
5½ x 8½, 16 pp, PB, 978-1-58023-085-8 **$4.95**

Twelve Steps

Recovery—The Sacred Art: The Twelve Steps as Spiritual Practice
By Rami Shapiro; Foreword by Joan Borysenko, PhD
Draws on insights and practices of different religious traditions to help you move more deeply into the universal spirituality of the Twelve Step system.
5½ x 8½, 240 pp, Quality PB Original, 978-1-59473-259-1 **$16.99**
(A book from SkyLight Paths, Jewish Lights' sister imprint)

100 Blessings Every Day: Daily Twelve Step Recovery Affirmations, Exercises for Personal Growth & Renewal Reflecting Seasons of the Jewish Year *By Rabbi Kerry M. Olitzky; Foreword by Rabbi Neil Gillman, PhD*
4½ x 6½, 432 pp, Quality PB, 978-1-879045-30-9 **$16.99**

Recovery from Codependence: A Jewish Twelve Steps Guide to Healing Your Soul
By Rabbi Kerry M. Olitzky 6 x 9, 160 pp, Quality PB, 978-1-879045-32-3 **$13.95**

Twelve Jewish Steps to Recovery, 2nd Edition: A Personal Guide to Turning from Alcoholism & Other Addictions—Drugs, Food, Gambling, Sex...
By Rabbi Kerry M. Olitzky and Stuart A. Copans, MD; Preface by Abraham J. Twerski, MD
6 x 9, 160 pp, Quality PB, 978-1-58023-409-2 **$16.99**

Social Justice

Where Justice Dwells
A Hands-On Guide to Doing Social Justice in Your Jewish Community
By Rabbi Jill Jacobs; Foreword by Rabbi David Saperstein
Provides ways to envision and act on your own ideals of social justice.
7 x 9, 288 pp, Quality PB Original, 978-1-58023-453-5 **$24.99**

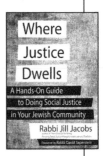

There Shall Be No Needy
Pursuing Social Justice through Jewish Law and Tradition
By Rabbi Jill Jacobs; Foreword by Rabbi Elliot N. Dorff, PhD; Preface by Simon Greer
Confronts the most pressing issues of twenty-first-century America from a deeply
Jewish perspective. 6 x 9, 288 pp, Quality PB, 978-1-58023-425-2 **$16.99**

There Shall Be No Needy Teacher's Guide 8½ x 11, 56 pp, PB, 978-1-58023-429-0 **$8.99**

Conscience
The Duty to Obey and the Duty to Disobey
By Rabbi Harold M. Schulweis
Examines the idea of conscience and the role conscience plays in our relationships
to government, law, ethics, religion, human nature, God—and to each other.
6 x 9, 160 pp, Quality PB, 978-1-58023-419-1 **$16.99**; HC, 978-1-58023-375-0 **$19.99**

Judaism and Justice
The Jewish Passion to Repair the World
By Rabbi Sidney Schwarz; Foreword by Ruth Messinger
Explores the relationship between Judaism, social justice and the Jewish identity
of American Jews. 6 x 9, 352 pp, Quality PB, 978-1-58023-353-8 **$19.99**

Spirituality / Women's Interest

New Jewish Feminism
Probing the Past, Forging the Future
Edited by Rabbi Elyse Goldstein; Foreword by Anita Diamant
Looks at the growth and accomplishments of Jewish feminism and what they
mean for Jewish women today and tomorrow.
6 x 9, 480 pp, HC, 978-1-58023-359-0 **$24.99**

The Divine Feminine in Biblical Wisdom Literature
Selections Annotated & Explained
Translation & Annotation by Rabbi Rami Shapiro
5½ x 8½, 240 pp, Quality PB, 978-1-59473-109-9 **$16.99**
(A book from SkyLight Paths, Jewish Lights' sister imprint)

The Quotable Jewish Woman
Wisdom, Inspiration & Humor from the Mind & Heart
Edited by Elaine Bernstein Partnow
6 x 9, 496 pp, Quality PB, 978-1-58023-236-4 **$19.99**

The Women's Haftarah Commentary
New Insights from Women Rabbis on the 54 Weekly Haftarah Portions,
the 5 Megillot & Special Shabbatot
Edited by Rabbi Elyse Goldstein
Illuminates the historical significance of female portrayals in the Haftarah and the
Five Megillot. 6 x 9, 560 pp, Quality PB, 978-1-58023-371-2 **$19.99**

The Women's Torah Commentary
New Insights from Women Rabbis on the 54 Weekly Torah Portions
Edited by Rabbi Elyse Goldstein
Over fifty women rabbis offer inspiring insights on the Torah, in a week-by-week format.
6 x 9, 496 pp, Quality PB, 978-1-58023-370-5 **$19.99**; HC, 978-1-58023-076-6 **$34.95**

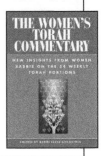

See Passover for *The Women's Passover Companion: Women's Reflections on the Festival of
Freedom* and *The Women's Seder Sourcebook: Rituals & Readings for Use at the Passover Seder.*

Judaism / Christianity / Interfaith

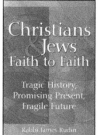

Christians & Jews—Faith to Faith: Tragic History, Promising Present, Fragile Future *By Rabbi James Rudin*
A probing examination of Christian-Jewish relations that looks at the major issues facing both faith communities. 6 x 9, 288 pp, HC, 978-1-58023-432-0 **$24.99**

Religion Gone Astray: What We Found at the Heart of Interfaith
By Pastor Don Mackenzie, Rabbi Ted Falcon and Imam Jamal Rahman
Probes more deeply into the problem aspects of our religious institutions—specifically exclusivity, violence, inequality of men and women, and homophobia—to provide a profound understanding of the nature of what divides us.
6 x 9, 192 pp, Quality PB, 978-1-59473-317-8 **$16.99***

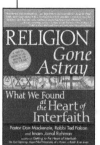

Getting to the Heart of Interfaith: The Eye-Opening, Hope-Filled Friendship of a Pastor, a Rabbi and an Imam
By Rabbi Ted Falcon, Pastor Don Mackenzie and Imam Jamal Rahman
Presents ways we can work together to transcend the differences that have divided us historically. 6 x 9, 192 pp, Quality PB, 978-1-59473-263-8 **$16.99***

How to Do Good & Avoid Evil: A Global Ethic from the Sources of Judaism
By Hans Küng and Rabbi Walter Homolka 6 x 9, 224 pp, HC, 978-1-59473-255-3 **$19.99***

Claiming Earth as Common Ground: The Ecological Crisis through the Lens of Faith *By Rabbi Andrea Cohen-Kiener* 6 x 9, 192 pp, Quality PB, 978-1-59473-261-4 **$16.99***

Modern Jews Engage the New Testament: Enhancing Jewish Well-Being in a Christian Environment *By Rabbi Michael J. Cook, PhD* 6 x 9, 416 pp, HC, 978-1-58023-313-2 **$29.99**

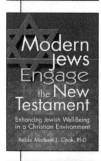

The Changing Christian World: A Brief Introduction for Jews
By Rabbi Leonard A. Schoolman 5½ x 8½, 176 pp, Quality PB, 978-1-58023-344-6 **$16.99**

Christians & Jews in Dialogue: Learning in the Presence of the Other
By Mary C. Boys and Sara S. Lee
6 x 9, 240 pp, Quality PB, 978-1-59473-254-6 **$18.99**; HC, 978-1-59473-144-0 **21.99***

Disaster Spiritual Care: Practical Clergy Responses to Community, Regional and National Tragedy *Edited by Rabbi Stephen B. Roberts, BCJC, and Rev. Willard W. C. Ashley Sr., DMin, DH*
6 x 9, 384 pp, HC, 978-1-59473-240-9 **$40.00***

How to Be a Perfect Stranger, 5th Edition: The Essential Religious Etiquette Handbook *Edited by Stuart M. Matlins and Arthur J. Magida*
6 x 9, 432 pp, Quality PB, 978-1-59473-294-2 **$19.99***

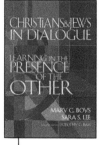

InterActive Faith: The Essential Interreligious Community-Building Handbook
Edited by Rev. Bud Heckman with Rori Picker Neiss
6 x 9, 304 pp, Quality PB, 978-1-59473-273-7 **$16.99**; HC, 978-1-59473-237-9 **$29.99***

Introducing My Faith and My Community
The Jewish Outreach Institute Guide for the Christian in a Jewish Interfaith Relationship
By Rabbi Kerry M. Olitzky 6 x 9, 176 pp, Quality PB, 978-1-58023-192-3 **$16.99**

The Jewish Approach to Repairing the World (*Tikkun Olam*)
A Brief Introduction for Christians *By Rabbi Elliot N. Dorff, PhD, with Rev. Cory Willson*
5½ x 8½, 256 pp, Quality PB, 978-1-58023-349-1 **$16.99**

The Jewish Connection to Israel, the Promised Land: A Brief Introduction for Christians *By Rabbi Eugene Korn, PhD* 5½ x 8½, 192 pp, Quality PB, 978-1-58023-318-7 **$14.99**

Jewish Holidays: A Brief Introduction for Christians *By Rabbi Kerry M. Olitzky and Rabbi Daniel Judson* 5½ x 8½, 176 pp, Quality PB, 978-1-58023-302-6 **$16.99**

Jewish Ritual: A Brief Introduction for Christians *By Rabbi Kerry M. Olitzky and Rabbi Daniel Judson* 5½ x 8½, 144 pp, Quality PB, 978-1-58023-210-4 **$14.99**

A Jewish Understanding of the New Testament *By Rabbi Samuel Sandmel; Preface by Rabbi David Sandmel* 5½ x 8½, 368 pp, Quality PB, 978-1-59473-048-1 **$19.99***

Righteous Gentiles in the Hebrew Bible: Ancient Role Models for Sacred Relationships *By Rabbi Jeffrey K. Salkin; Foreword by Rabbi Harold M. Schulweis; Preface by Phyllis Tickle*
6 x 9, 192 pp, Quality PB, 978-1-58023-364-4 **$18.99**

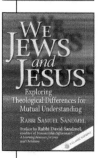

We Jews and Jesus: Exploring Theological Differences for Mutual Understanding
By Rabbi Samuel Sandmel; Preface by Rabbi David Sandmel
6 x 9, 192 pp, Quality PB, 978-1-59473-208-9 **$16.99**

*A book from SkyLight Paths, Jewish Lights' sister imprint

Meditation

Jewish Meditation Practices for Everyday Life
Awakening Your Heart, Connecting with God
By Rabbi Jeff Roth
Offers a fresh take on meditation that draws on life experience and living life with greater clarity as opposed to the traditional method of rigorous study.
6 x 9, 224 pp, Quality PB, 978-1-58023-397-2 **$18.99**

The Handbook of Jewish Meditation Practices
A Guide for Enriching the Sabbath and Other Days of Your Life
By Rabbi David A. Cooper Easy-to-learn meditation techniques.
6 x 9, 208 pp, Quality PB, 978-1-58023-102-2 **$16.95**

Discovering Jewish Meditation, 2nd Edition
Instruction & Guidance for Learning an Ancient Spiritual Practice
By Nan Fink Gefen, PhD 6 x 9, 208 pp, Quality PB, 978-1-58023-462-7 **$16.99**

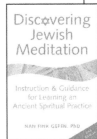

Meditation from the Heart of Judaism
Today's Teachers Share Their Practices, Techniques, and Faith
Edited by Avram Davis 6 x 9, 256 pp, Quality PB, 978-1-58023-049-0 **$16.95**

Ritual / Sacred Practices

The Jewish Dream Book: The Key to Opening the Inner Meaning of
Your Dreams *By Vanessa L. Ochs, PhD, with Elizabeth Ochs; Illus. by Kristina Swarner*
Instructions for how modern people can perform ancient Jewish dream practices and dream interpretations drawn from the Jewish wisdom tradition.
8 x 8, 128 pp, Full-color illus., Deluxe PB w/ flaps, 978-1-58023-132-9 **$16.95**

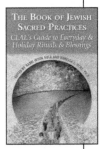

God in Your Body: Kabbalah, Mindfulness and Embodied Spiritual Practice
By Jay Michaelson
The first comprehensive treatment of the body in Jewish spiritual practice and an essential guide to the sacred.
6 x 9, 272 pp, Quality PB, 978-1-58023-304-0 **$18.99**

The Book of Jewish Sacred Practices: CLAL's Guide to Everyday &
Holiday Rituals & Blessings *Edited by Rabbi Irwin Kula and Vanessa L. Ochs, PhD*
6 x 9, 368 pp, Quality PB, 978-1-58023-152-7 **$18.95**

Jewish Ritual: A Brief Introduction for Christians
By Rabbi Kerry M. Olitzky and Rabbi Daniel Judson
5½ x 8½, 144 pp, Quality PB, 978-1-58023-210-4 **$14.99**

The Rituals & Practices of a Jewish Life: A Handbook for Personal Spiritual
Renewal *Edited by Rabbi Kerry M. Olitzky and Rabbi Daniel Judson*
6 x 9, 272 pp, Illus., Quality PB, 978-1-58023-169-5 **$18.95**

The Sacred Art of Lovingkindness: Preparing to Practice
By Rabbi Rami Shapiro 5½ x 8½, 176 pp, Quality PB, 978-1-59473-151-8 **$16.99**
(A book from SkyLight Paths, Jewish Lights' sister imprint)

Science Fiction / Mystery & Detective Fiction

Criminal Kabbalah: An Intriguing Anthology of Jewish Mystery &
Detective Fiction *Edited by Lawrence W. Raphael; Foreword by Laurie R. King*
All-new stories from twelve of today's masters of mystery and detective fiction—sure to delight mystery buffs of all faith traditions.
6 x 9, 256 pp, Quality PB, 978-1-58023-109-1 **$16.95**

Mystery Midrash: An Anthology of Jewish Mystery & Detective Fiction
Edited by Lawrence W. Raphael; Preface by Joel Siegel
6 x 9, 304 pp, Quality PB, 978-1-58023-055-1 **$16.95**

Wandering Stars: An Anthology of Jewish Fantasy & Science Fiction
Edited by Jack Dann; Introduction by Isaac Asimov
6 x 9, 272 pp, Quality PB, 978-1-58023-005-6 **$18.99**

More Wandering Stars: An Anthology of Outstanding Stories of Jewish Fantasy and
Science Fiction *Edited by Jack Dann; Introduction by Isaac Asimov*
6 x 9, 192 pp, Quality PB, 978-1-58023-063-6 **$16.95**

Theology / Philosophy / The Way Into... Series

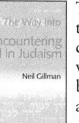

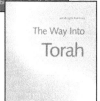

The Way Into... series offers an accessible and highly usable "guided tour" of the Jewish faith, people, history and beliefs—in total, an introduction to Judaism that will enable you to understand and interact with the sacred texts of the Jewish tradition. Each volume is written by a leading contemporary scholar and teacher, and explores one key aspect of Judaism. The Way Into... series enables all readers to achieve a real sense of Jewish cultural literacy through guided study.

The Way Into Encountering God in Judaism
By Rabbi Neil Gillman, PhD

For everyone who wants to understand how Jews have encountered God throughout history and today.

6 x 9, 240 pp, Quality PB, 978-1-58023-199-2 **$18.99**; HC, 978-1-58023-025-4 **$21.95**

Also Available: **The Jewish Approach to God:** A Brief Introduction for Christians
By Rabbi Neil Gillman, PhD

5½ x 8½, 192 pp, Quality PB, 978-1-58023-190-9 **$16.95**

The Way Into Jewish Mystical Tradition
By Rabbi Lawrence Kushner

Allows readers to interact directly with the sacred mystical texts of the Jewish tradition. An accessible introduction to the concepts of Jewish mysticism, their religious and spiritual significance, and how they relate to life today.

6 x 9, 224 pp, Quality PB, 978-1-58023-200-5 **$18.99**; HC, 978-1-58023-029-2 **$21.95**

The Way Into Jewish Prayer
By Rabbi Lawrence A. Hoffman, PhD

Opens the door to 3,000 years of Jewish prayer, making anyone feel at home in the Jewish way of communicating with God.

6 x 9, 208 pp, Quality PB, 978-1-58023-201-2 **$18.99**

The Way Into Jewish Prayer Teacher's Guide
By Rabbi Jennifer Ossakow Goldsmith

8½ x 11, 42 pp, PB, 978-1-58023-345-3 **$8.99**

Download a free copy at www.jewishlights.com.

The Way Into Judaism and the Environment
By Jeremy Benstein, PhD

Explores the ways in which Judaism contributes to contemporary social-environmental issues, the extent to which Judaism is part of the problem and how it can be part of the solution.

6 x 9, 288 pp, Quality PB, 978-1-58023-368-2 **$18.99**; HC, 978-1-58023-268-5 **$24.99**

The Way Into *Tikkun Olam* (Repairing the World)
By Rabbi Elliot N. Dorff, PhD

An accessible introduction to the Jewish concept of the individual's responsibility to care for others and repair the world.

6 x 9, 304 pp, Quality PB, 978-1-58023-328-6 **$18.99**

The Way Into Torah
By Rabbi Norman J. Cohen, PhD

Helps guide you in the exploration of the origins and development of Torah, explains why it should be studied and how to do it.

6 x 9, 176 pp, Quality PB, 978-1-58023-198-5 **$16.99**

The Way Into the Varieties of Jewishness
By Sylvia Barack Fishman, PhD

Explores the religious and historical understanding of what it has meant to be Jewish from ancient times to the present controversy over "Who is a Jew?"

6 x 9, 288 pp, Quality PB, 978-1-58023-367-5 **$18.99**; HC, 978-1-58023-030-8 **$24.99**

Theology / Philosophy

From Defender to Critic: The Search for a New Jewish Self
By Dr. David Hartman
A daring self-examination of Hartman's goals, which were not to strip halakha of its authority but to create a space for questioning and critique that allows for the traditionally religious Jew to act out a moral life in tune with modern experience.
6 x 9, 336 pp, HC, 978-1-58023-515-0 **$35.00**

Our Religious Brains: What Cognitive Science Reveals about Belief, Morality, Community and Our Relationship with God
By Rabbi Ralph D. Mecklenburger; Foreword by Dr. Howard Kelfer; Preface by Dr. Neil Gillman
This is a groundbreaking, accessible look at the implications of cognitive science for religion and theology, intended for laypeople.   6 x 9, 224 pp, HC, 978-1-58023-508-2 **$24.99**

The Other Talmud—*The Yerushalmi*: Unlocking the Secrets of The Talmud of Israel for Judaism Today   *By Rabbi Judith Z. Abrams, PhD*
A fascinating—and stimulating—look at "the other Talmud" and the possibilities for Jewish life reflected there.   6 x 9, 256 pp, HC, 978-1-58023-463-4 **$24.99**

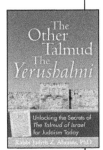

The Way of Man: According to Hasidic Teaching
By Martin Buber; New Translation and Introduction by Rabbi Bernard H. Mehlman and Dr. Gabriel E. Padawer; Foreword by Paul Mendes-Flohr
An accessible and engaging new translation of Buber's classic work—available as an e-book only.   E-book, 978-1-58023-601-0 Digital List Price **$14.99**

The Death of Death: Resurrection and Immortality in Jewish Thought
By Rabbi Neil Gillman, PhD   6 x 9, 336 pp, Quality PB, 978-1-58023-081-0 **$18.95**

Doing Jewish Theology: God, Torah & Israel in Modern Judaism   *By Rabbi Neil Gillman, PhD*
6 x 9, 304 pp, Quality PB, 978-1-58023-439-9 **$18.99**; HC, 978-1-58023-322-4 **$24.99**

A Heart of Many Rooms: Celebrating the Many Voices within Judaism
By Dr. David Hartman   6 x 9, 352 pp, Quality PB, 978-1-58023-156-5 **$19.95**

The God Who Hates Lies: Confronting & Rethinking Jewish Tradition
By Dr. David Hartman with Charlie Buckholtz   6 x 9, 208 pp, HC, 978-1-58023-455-9 **$24.99**

Jewish Theology in Our Time: A New Generation Explores the Foundations and Future of Jewish Belief   *Edited by Rabbi Elliot J. Cosgrove, PhD; Foreword by Rabbi David J. Wolpe; Preface by Rabbi Carole B. Balin, PhD*   6 x 9, 240 pp, HC, 978-1-58023-413-9 **$24.99**

Maimonides—Essential Teachings on Jewish Faith & Ethics: The Book of Knowledge & the Thirteen Principles of Faith—Annotated & Explained
Translation and Annotation by Rabbi Marc D. Angel, PhD
5½ x 8½, 224 pp, Quality PB Original, 978-1-59473-311-6 **$18.99***

Maimonides, Spinoza and Us: Toward an Intellectually Vibrant Judaism
By Rabbi Marc D. Angel, PhD   6 x 9, 224 pp, HC, 978-1-58023-411-5 **$24.99**

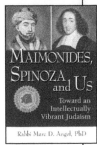

A Touch of the Sacred: A Theologian's Informal Guide to Jewish Belief
By Dr. Eugene B. Borowitz and Frances W. Schwartz
6 x 9, 256 pp, Quality PB, 978-1-58023-416-0 **$16.99**; HC, 978-1-58023-337-8 **$21.99**

Traces of God: Seeing God in Torah, History and Everyday Life   *By Rabbi Neil Gillman, PhD*
6 x 9, 240 pp, Quality PB, 978-1-58023-369-9 **$16.99**

Your Word Is Fire: The Hasidic Masters on Contemplative Prayer
Edited and translated by Rabbi Arthur Green, PhD, and Barry W. Holtz
6 x 9, 160 pp, Quality PB, 978-1-879045-25-5 **$16.99**

I Am Jewish
Personal Reflections Inspired by the Last Words of Daniel Pearl
Almost 150 Jews—both famous and not—from all walks of life, from all around the world, write about many aspects of their Judaism.
Edited by Judea and Ruth Pearl   6 x 9, 304 pp, Deluxe PB w/ flaps, 978-1-58023-259-3 **$18.99**
Download a free copy of the *I Am Jewish* Teacher's Guide at www.jewishlights.com.

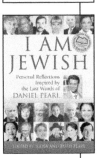

Hannah Senesh: Her Life and Diary, The First Complete Edition
By Hannah Senesh; Foreword by Marge Piercy; Preface by Eitan Senesh; Afterword by Roberta Grossman
6 x 9, 368 pp, b/w photos, Quality PB, 978-1-58023-342-2 **$19.99**

*A book from SkyLight Paths, Jewish Lights' sister imprint

Inspiration

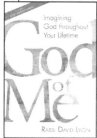

God of Me: Imagining God throughout Your Lifetime
By Rabbi David Lyon Helps you cut through preconceived ideas of God and dogmas that stifle your creativity when thinking about your personal relationship with God. 6 x 9, 176 pp, Quality PB, 978-1-58023-452-8 **$16.99**

The God Upgrade: Finding Your 21st-Century Spirituality in Judaism's 5,000-Year-Old Tradition *By Rabbi Jamie Korngold; Foreword by Rabbi Harold M. Schulweis* A provocative look at how our changing God concepts have shaped every aspect of Judaism. 6 x 9, 176 pp, Quality PB, 978-1-58023-443-6 **$15.99**

The Seven Questions You're Asked in Heaven: Reviewing and Renewing Your Life on Earth *By Dr. Ron Wolfson* An intriguing and entertaining resource for living a life that matters. 6 x 9, 176 pp, Quality PB, 978-1-58023-407-8 **$16.99**

Happiness and the Human Spirit: The Spirituality of Becoming the Best You Can Be *By Rabbi Abraham J. Twerski, MD*
Shows you that true happiness is attainable once you stop looking outside yourself for the source. 6 x 9, 176 pp, Quality PB, 978-1-58023-404-7 **$16.99**; HC, 978-1-58023-343-9 **$19.99**

A Formula for Proper Living: Practical Lessons from Life and Torah
By Rabbi Abraham J. Twerski, MD 6 x 9, 144 pp, HC, 978-1-58023-402-3 **$19.99**

The Bridge to Forgiveness: Stories and Prayers for Finding God and Restoring Wholeness *By Rabbi Karyn D. Kedar* 6 x 9, 176 pp, Quality PB, 978-1-58023-451-1 **$16.99**

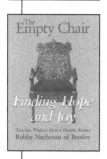

The Empty Chair: Finding Hope and Joy—Timeless Wisdom from a Hasidic Master, Rebbe Nachman of Breslov *Adapted by Moshe Mykoff and the Breslov Research Institute*
4 x 6, 128 pp, Deluxe PB w/ flaps, 978-1-879045-67-5 **$9.99**

The Gentle Weapon: Prayers for Everyday and Not-So-Everyday Moments—Timeless Wisdom from the Teachings of the Hasidic Master, Rebbe Nachman of Breslov *Adapted by Moshe Mykoff and S. C. Mizrahi, together with the Breslov Research Institute*
4 x 6, 144 pp, Deluxe PB w/ flaps, 978-1-58023-022-3 **$9.99**

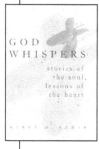

God Whispers: Stories of the Soul, Lessons of the Heart *By Rabbi Karyn D. Kedar*
6 x 9, 176 pp, Quality PB, 978-1-58023-088-9 **$15.95**

God's To-Do List: 103 Ways to Be an Angel and Do God's Work on Earth
By Dr. Ron Wolfson 6 x 9, 144 pp, Quality PB, 978-1-58023-301-9 **$16.99**

Jewish Stories from Heaven and Earth: Inspiring Tales to Nourish the Heart and Soul *Edited by Rabbi Dov Peretz Elkins* 6 x 9, 304 pp, Quality PB, 978-1-58023-363-7 **$16.99**

Life's Daily Blessings: Inspiring Reflections on Gratitude and Joy for Every Day, Based on Jewish Wisdom *By Rabbi Kerry M. Olitzky* 4½ x 6½, 368 pp, Quality PB, 978-1-58023-396-5 **$16.99**

Restful Reflections: Nighttime Inspiration to Calm the Soul, Based on Jewish Wisdom
By Rabbi Kerry M. Olitzky and Rabbi Lori Forman-Jacobi 5 x 8, 352 pp, Quality PB, 978-1-58023-091-9 **$16.99**

Sacred Intentions: Morning Inspiration to Strengthen the Spirit, Based on Jewish Wisdom
By Rabbi Kerry M. Olitzky and Rabbi Lori Forman-Jacobi 4½ x 6¼, 448 pp, Quality PB, 978-1-58023-061-2 **$16.99**

Kabbalah / Mysticism

Jewish Mysticism and the Spiritual Life: Classical Texts, Contemporary Reflections *Edited by Dr. Lawrence Fine, Dr. Eitan Fishbane and Rabbi Or N. Rose* Inspirational and thought-provoking materials for contemplation, discussion and action. 6 x 9, 256 pp, HC, 978-1-58023-434-4 **$24.99**

Ehyeh: A Kabbalah for Tomorrow
By Rabbi Arthur Green, PhD 6 x 9, 224 pp, Quality PB, 978-1-58023-213-5 **$18.99**

The Gift of Kabbalah: Discovering the Secrets of Heaven, Renewing Your Life on Earth
By Tamar Frankiel, PhD 6 x 9, 256 pp, Quality PB, 978-1-58023-141-1 **$16.95**

Seek My Face: A Jewish Mystical Theology *By Rabbi Arthur Green, PhD*
6 x 9, 304 pp, Quality PB, 978-1-58023-130-5 **$19.95**

Zohar: Annotated & Explained *Translation & Annotation by Dr. Daniel C. Matt; Foreword by Andrew Harvey* 5½ x 8½, 176 pp, Quality PB, 978-1-893361-51-5 **$16.99**
(A book from SkyLight Paths, Jewish Lights' sister imprint)

See also *The Way Into Jewish Mystical Tradition* in The Way Into... Series.

Spirituality

The Jewish Lights Spirituality Handbook: A Guide to Understanding, Exploring & Living a Spiritual Life *Edited by Stuart M. Matlins*
What exactly is "Jewish" about spirituality? How do I make it a part of my life? Fifty of today's foremost spiritual leaders share their ideas and experience with us.
6 x 9, 456 pp, Quality PB, 978-1-58023-093-3 **$19.99**

The Sabbath Soul: Mystical Reflections on the Transformative Power of Holy Time *Selection, Translation and Commentary by Eitan Fishbane, PhD*
Explores the writings of mystical masters of Hasidism. Provides translations and interpretations of a wide range of Hasidic sources previously unavailable in English that reflect the spiritual transformation that takes place on the seventh day.
6 x 9, 208 pp, Quality PB, 978-1-58023-459-7 **$18.99**

Repentance: The Meaning and Practice of *Teshuvah*
By Dr. Louis E. Newman; Foreword by Rabbi Harold M. Schulweis; Preface by Rabbi Karyn D. Kedar
Examines both the practical and philosophical dimensions of *teshuvah*, Judaism's core religious-moral teaching on repentance, and its value for us—Jews and non-Jews alike—today. 6 x 9, 256 pp, HC, 978-1-58023-426-9 **$24.99**

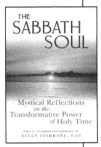

Aleph-Bet Yoga: Embodying the Hebrew Letters for Physical and Spiritual Well-Being
By Steven A. Rapp; Foreword by Tamar Frankiel, PhD, and Judy Greenfeld; Preface by Hart Lazer
7 x 10, 128 pp, b/w photos, Quality PB, Lay-flat binding, 978-1-58023-162-6 **$16.95**

A Book of Life: Embracing Judaism as a Spiritual Practice
By Rabbi Michael Strassfeld 6 x 9, 544 pp, Quality PB, 978-1-58023-247-0 **$19.99**

Bringing the Psalms to Life: How to Understand and Use the Book of Psalms
By Rabbi Daniel F. Polish, PhD 6 x 9, 208 pp, Quality PB, 978-1-58023-157-2 **$16.95**

Does the Soul Survive? A Jewish Journey to Belief in Afterlife, Past Lives & Living with Purpose *By Rabbi Elie Kaplan Spitz; Foreword by Brian L. Weiss, MD*
6 x 9, 288 pp, Quality PB, 978-1-58023-165-7 **$18.99**

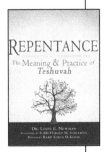

Entering the Temple of Dreams: Jewish Prayers, Movements and Meditations for the End of the Day *By Tamar Frankiel, PhD, and Judy Greenfeld*
7 x 10, 192 pp, illus., Quality PB, 978-1-58023-079-7 **$16.95**

First Steps to a New Jewish Spirit: Reb Zalman's Guide to Recapturing the Intimacy & Ecstasy in Your Relationship with God *By Rabbi Zalman M. Schachter-Shalomi with Donald Gropman* 6 x 9, 144 pp, Quality PB, 978-1-58023-182-4 **$16.95**

Foundations of Sephardic Spirituality: The Inner Life of Jews of the Ottoman Empire
By Rabbi Marc D. Angel, PhD 6 x 9, 224 pp, Quality PB, 978-1-58023-341-5 **$18.99**

God & the Big Bang: Discovering Harmony between Science & Spirituality
By Dr. Daniel C. Matt 6 x 9, 216 pp, Quality PB, 978-1-879045-89-7 **$18.99**

God in Our Relationships: Spirituality between People from the Teachings of Martin Buber *By Rabbi Dennis S. Ross* 5½ x 8½, 160 pp, Quality PB, 978-1-58023-147-3 **$16.95**

Judaism, Physics and God: Searching for Sacred Metaphors in a Post-Einstein World
By Rabbi David W. Nelson 6 x 9, 352 pp, Quality PB, inc. reader's discussion guide,
978-1-58023-306-4 **$18.99**; HC, 352 pp, 978-1-58023-252-4 **$24.99**

Meaning & Mitzvah: Daily Practices for Reclaiming Judaism through Prayer, God, Torah, Hebrew, Mitzvot and Peoplehood *By Rabbi Goldie Milgram*
7 x 9, 336 pp, Quality PB, 978-1-58023-256-2 **$19.99**

Minding the Temple of the Soul: Balancing Body, Mind, and Spirit through Traditional Jewish Prayer, Movement, and Meditation *By Tamar Frankiel, PhD, and Judy Greenfeld*
7 x 10, 184 pp, Illus., Quality PB, 978-1-879045-64-4 **$18.99**

One God Clapping: The Spiritual Path of a Zen Rabbi *By Rabbi Alan Lew with Sherril Jaffe*
5½ x 8½, 336 pp, Quality PB, 978-1-58023-115-2 **$16.95**

The Soul of the Story: Meetings with Remarkable People
By Rabbi David Zeller 6 x 9, 288 pp, HC, 978-1-58023-272-2 **$21.99**

Tanya, the Masterpiece of Hasidic Wisdom: Selections Annotated & Explained
Translation & Annotation by Rabbi Rami Shapiro; Foreword by Rabbi Zalman M. Schachter-Shalomi
5½ x 8½, 240 pp, Quality PB, 978-1-59473-275-1 **$16.99**

These Are the Words, 2nd Edition: A Vocabulary of Jewish Spiritual Life
By Rabbi Arthur Green, PhD 6 x 9, 320 pp, Quality PB, 978-1-58023-494-8 **$19.99**

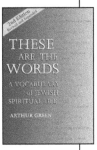

Spirituality / Prayer

Making Prayer Real: Leading Jewish Spiritual Voices on Why Prayer Is Difficult and What to Do about It *By Rabbi Mike Comins*
A new and different response to the challenges of Jewish prayer, with "best prayer practices" from Jewish spiritual leaders of all denominations.
6 x 9, 320 pp, Quality PB, 978-1-58023-417-7 **$18.99**

Witnesses to the One: The Spiritual History of the *Sh'ma*
By Rabbi Joseph B. Meszler; Foreword by Rabbi Elyse Goldstein
6 x 9, 176 pp, Quality PB, 978-1-58023-400-9 **$16.99**; HC, 978-1-58023-309-5 **$19.99**

My People's Prayer Book Series: Traditional Prayers, Modern Commentaries *Edited by Rabbi Lawrence A. Hoffman, PhD*
Provides diverse and exciting commentary to the traditional liturgy. Will help you find new wisdom in Jewish prayer, and bring liturgy into your life. Each book includes Hebrew text, modern translations and commentaries from all perspectives of the Jewish world.

Vol. 1—The *Sh'ma* and Its Blessings
  7 x 10, 168 pp, HC, 978-1-879045-79-8 **$29.99**
Vol. 2—The *Amidah* 7 x 10, 240 pp, HC, 978-1-879045-80-4 **$24.95**
Vol. 3—*P'sukei D'zimrah* (Morning Psalms)
  7 x 10, 240 pp, HC, 978-1-879045-81-1 **$29.99**
Vol. 4—*Seder K'riat Hatorah* (The Torah Service)
  7 x 10, 264 pp, HC, 978-1-879045-82-8 **$29.99**
Vol. 5—*Birkhot Hashachar* (Morning Blessings)
  7 x 10, 240 pp, HC, 978-1-879045-83-5 **$24.95**
Vol. 6—*Tachanun* and Concluding Prayers
  7 x 10, 240 pp, HC, 978-1-879045-84-2 **$24.95**
Vol. 7—Shabbat at Home 7 x 10, 240 pp, HC, 978-1-879045-85-9 **$24.95**
Vol. 8—*Kabbalat Shabbat* (Welcoming Shabbat in the Synagogue)
  7 x 10, 240 pp, HC, 978-1-58023-121-3 **$24.99**
Vol. 9—Welcoming the Night: *Minchah* and *Ma'ariv* (Afternoon and
  Evening Prayer) 7 x 10, 272 pp, HC, 978-1-58023-262-3 **$24.99**
Vol. 10—Shabbat Morning: *Shacharit* and *Musaf* (Morning and
  Additional Services) 7 x 10, 240 pp, HC, 978-1-58023-240-1 **$29.99**

Spirituality / Lawrence Kushner

I'm God; You're Not: Observations on Organized Religion & Other Disguises of the Ego
6 x 9, 256 pp, Quality PB, 978-1-58023-513-6 **$18.99**; HC, 978-1-58023-441-2 **$21.99**

The Book of Letters: A Mystical Hebrew Alphabet
Popular HC Edition, 6 x 9, 80 pp, 2-color text, 978-1-879045-00-2 **$24.95**
Collector's Limited Edition, 9 x 12, 80 pp, gold-foil-embossed pages, w/ limited-edition silkscreened print, 978-1-879045-04-0 **$349.00**

The Book of Miracles: A Young Person's Guide to Jewish Spiritual Awareness
6 x 9, 96 pp, 2-color illus., HC, 978-1-879045-78-1 **$16.95** *For ages 9–13*

The Book of Words: Talking Spiritual Life, Living Spiritual Talk
6 x 9, 160 pp, Quality PB, 978-1-58023-020-9 **$18.99**

Eyes Remade for Wonder: A Lawrence Kushner Reader *Introduction by Thomas Moore*
6 x 9, 240 pp, Quality PB, 978-1-58023-042-1 **$18.95**

God Was in This Place & I, i Did Not Know: Finding Self, Spirituality and
Ultimate Meaning 6 x 9, 192 pp, Quality PB, 978-1-879045-33-0 **$16.95**

Honey from the Rock: An Introduction to Jewish Mysticism
6 x 9, 176 pp, Quality PB, 978-1-58023-073-5 **$16.95**

Invisible Lines of Connection: Sacred Stories of the Ordinary
5½ x 8½, 160 pp, Quality PB, 978-1-879045-98-9 **$16.99**

Jewish Spirituality: A Brief Introduction for Christians
5½ x 8½, 112 pp, Quality PB, 978-1-58023-150-3 **$12.95**

The River of Light: Jewish Mystical Awareness
6 x 9, 192 pp, Quality PB, 978-1-58023-096-4 **$18.99**

The Way Into Jewish Mystical Tradition
6 x 9, 224 pp, Quality PB, 978-1-58023-200-5 **$18.99**; HC, 978-1-58023-029-2 **$21.95**

About Jewish Lights

People of all faiths and backgrounds yearn for books that attract, engage, educate, and spiritually inspire.

Our principal goal is to stimulate thought and help all people learn about who the Jewish People are, where they come from, and what the future can be made to hold. While people of our diverse Jewish heritage are the primary audience, our books speak to people in the Christian world as well and will broaden their understanding of Judaism and the roots of their own faith.

We bring to you authors who are at the forefront of spiritual thought and experience. While each has something different to say, they all say it in a voice that you can hear.

Our books are designed to welcome you and then to engage, stimulate, and inspire. We judge our success not only by whether or not our books are beautiful and commercially successful, but by whether or not they make a difference in your life.

For your information and convenience, at the back of this book we have provided a list of other Jewish Lights books you might find interesting and useful. They cover all the categories of your life:

Bar/Bat Mitzvah
Bible Study / Midrash
Children's Books
Congregation Resources
Current Events / History
Ecology / Environment
Fiction: Mystery, Science Fiction
Grief / Healing
Holidays / Holy Days
Inspiration
Kabbalah / Mysticism / Enneagram

Life Cycle
Meditation
Men's Interest
Parenting
Prayer / Ritual / Sacred Practice
Social Justice
Spirituality
Theology / Philosophy
Travel
Twelve Steps
Women's Interest

Stuart M. Matlins, Publisher

RABBI SHEFA GOLD is director of C-DEEP: The Center for Devotional, Energy and Ecstatic Practice in Jemez Springs, New Mexico. Shefa composes and performs spiritual music, has produced several recordings, and her liturgies have been published in many prayer books. She teaches workshops and retreats on the theory and art of chanting, devotional healing, spiritual community building and meditation around the world. She also trains chant leaders in Kol Zimra, a two-year program for rabbis, cantors and lay leaders. Shefa, who is on the faculty of the Institute for Jewish Spirituality, combines her grounding in Judaism with a background in Buddhist, Christian, Islamic and Native American spiritual traditions to make her uniquely qualified as a spiritual bridge celebrating the shared path of devotion. She is author of *Torah Journeys: The Inner Path to the Promised Land* and *In the Fever of Love: An Illumination of the Song of Songs*. For more information about Rabbi Shefa Gold, please visit her website at www.RabbiShefaGold.com.

Praise for *The Magic of Hebrew Chant*

"Incredibly clear, valuable.... A sacred book to savor and widely gift to family, students and friends."
—**Rabbi Goldie Milgram**, author, *Meaning & Mitzvah: Daily Practices for Reclaiming Judaism through Prayer, God, Torah, Hebrew, Mitzvot and Peoplehood*

"Invites the reader of any spiritual path to enter more deeply into the heart of love."
—**The Rev. Robert Corin Morris, DD**, founder, Interweave, Inc.

"Allows readers to inhabit the immersive, transformative, gently flowering yet powerful world of chant: an indispensable guide for the spiritual seeker of our time. Highly recommended!"
—**Rabbi Nehemia Polen, PhD**, professor of Jewish thought, Hebrew College

"Transforms the world of chant, allowing both the chanter and the listener to find personal meaning in Jewish prayer through the mesmerizing repetitions of words and meditative melody."
—**Cantor Linda Hirschhorn**

"A tour de force.... A luminous resource for the renewal of Jewish religious life and contemporary spirituality."
—**Rabbi Sheila Peltz Weinberg**, Institute for Jewish Spirituality

"Wise, warm advice from the foremost expert in this form of Jewish devotional practice. It is encyclopedic, thoughtful, accessible and deep."
—**Jay Michaelson, PhD**, author, *God in Your Body: Kabbalah, Mindfulness & Embodied Spiritual Practice*

"A deeply important contribution to all those interested in contemplative practice."
—**Rabbi Jeff Roth**, author, *Jewish Meditation Practices for Everyday Life: Awakening Your Heart, Connecting with God*

"[Will] awaken nothing less than a transformation in your self-understanding and love for others. The profound wisdom and amazingly beautiful chants are a gift for human flourishing. Be prepared to be touched by a magician of the soul."
—**Rabbi Irwin Kula**, coeditor, *The Book of Jewish Sacred Practices: Clal's Guide to Everyday & Holiday Rituals & Blessings*

"A treasure of exquisite simplicity, wisdom and love! With mellifluous and stunning beauty ... offers a path of awakening through which outworn habits of heart and mind are discarded, core truths rediscovered and ever more expansive capacity for joy is born."
—**Rabbi Marcia Prager**, author, *The Path of Blessing: Experiencing the Energy and Abundance of the Divine*

For People of All Faiths, All Backgrounds
JEWISH LIGHTS Publishing

4507 Charlotte Avenue, Suite 100
Nashville, TN 37209
Tel: (615) 255-2665

www.jewishlights.com

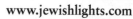
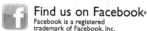
Find us on Facebook®
Facebook is a registered trademark of Facebook, Inc.

Printed in the USA
CPSIA information can be obtained
at www.ICGtesting.com
JSHW060046150824
68134JS00031B/2647